Theme for a D‌ay

by
Lisa Rogulic-Newsome

illustrated by Kathryn Hyndman

Cover by Kathryn Hyndman

Copyright © Good Apple, Inc., 1990

Good Apple, Inc.
1204 Buchanan St., Box 299
Carthage, IL 62321-0299

Copyright © Good Apple, Inc., 1990

ISBN No. 0-86653-545-4

Printing No. 9876543

Good Apple, Inc.
1204 Buchanan St., Box 299
Carthage, IL 62321-0299

Dedication

This book is fondly dedicated to my very special grand-mother, whose total faith in my abilities and creativity was never ending; to my husband, John, whose constant brainstorming and collaborating saw me through all the good times and even some bad; and to all those wonderfully creative students and teachers who are in need of that "little extra something" to help them rejuvenate and challenge their learning flames to keep on burning. Thank you all for being a part of keeping my mental light bulb aglow and my imagination forever young.

GA1154

Table of Contents

GA1154

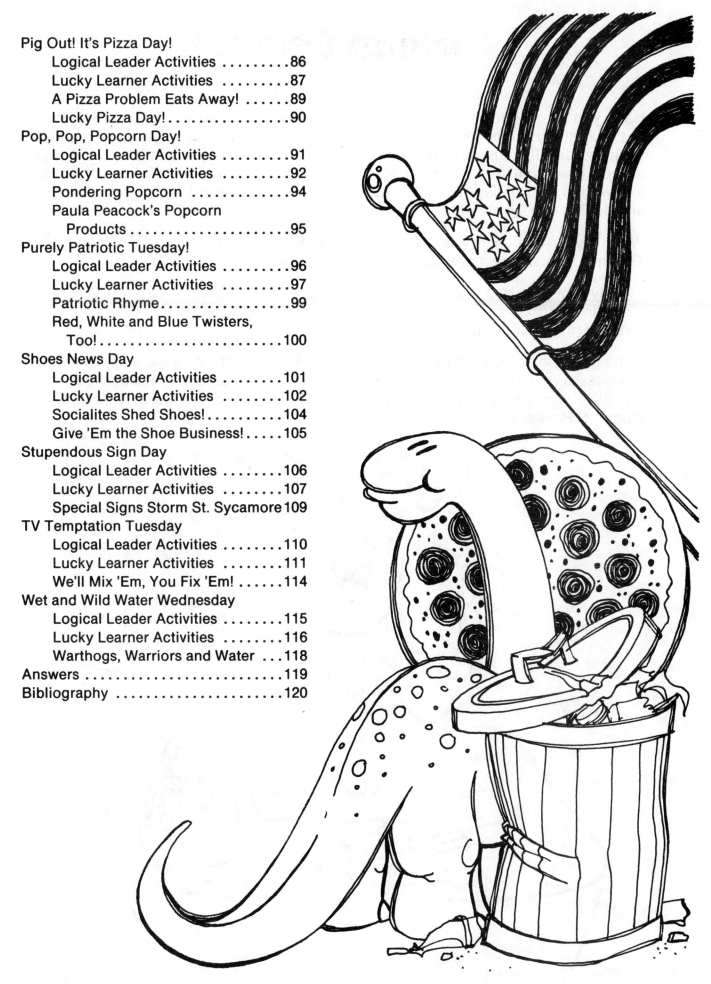

GA1154

Introduction

Have you ever gotten tired of the same old classroom routine, day in and day out? Has always presenting reading first, writing second, math third, science fourth, social studies fifth and art whenever you get a chance, every single day, five days a week, made you yearn for a change? Ever wonder what it might be like to create a new kind of "holiday" for kids, one which was really worth looking forward to and getting excited about?

Well, if your response was "yes" to any of those questions, then *Theme for a Day* may be just the answer you've been looking for!

Twenty-four different themes are presented which include a variety of multi-disciplinary tasks, stressing creativity and problem solving, and dealing with all levels of higher order thinking skills.

Don't go another year without the promise of some relief along the way! Choose those tasks which will suit your needs and fill your days with variety and excitement. You'll be surprised at how much you enjoy *Theme for a Day* as much as your students! Have a great time!

GA1154

An Array, More Than One Way to Use a *Theme for a Day*

Teachers, there are a variety of methods in which the ideas presented in this book can be utilized. Employ just one idea, or have a ball and use them all! Don't feel restricted to use the ideas offered here, though. Stretch your imagination and you'll be amazed at how inventive you can be in creating your very own *Theme for a Day* tasks.

Submitted below are just a few options for possible adaptation. Whichever alternative(s) you do choose, you'll have a wonderful time with your students because *Theme for a Day* really is a new learning craze!

1. Read through the different Logical Leader tasks, Lucky Learner tasks and supplemental action handouts and select as many as you feel will comfortably fill one of your school days, meet the needs of your students, and which can be satisfactorily accomplished within the confines of your physical area while using the materials at hand. Some activities also require more preparation than others so you may want to take this into consideration.

2. Extend the *Theme for a Day* activities to cover a week or two weeks' time, or even over the course of a month. Complete one or more of the various activities a day, and compile a class book containing samples of your students' work evolving around the theme.

GA1154

3. Pose the *Theme for a Day* activities to small groups to explore and complete, and ask the groups to share their finished products with the class.

4. Use the *Theme for a Day* activities to construct learning centers. Write the Lucky Learner tasks on activity cards in the shapes of items which relate to the theme. Cover a box or panel board with gift wrap which also symbolizes the theme, hang it with curtain hooks, punch holes in the activity cards and hang them on the box. Students can complete the tasks as independent study projects after their regular work has been completed or as enrichment for a unit the class is studying.

5. Use activities from all the *Theme for a Day* pages to add spice to your everyday routine throughout the year.

6. Anytime there is a lag in your schedule or a substitute is coming to take your place, use the *Theme for a Day* tasks as fillers to make lesson planning easier and your routine day more exciting.

GA1154

Banana Bonanza Day

Logical Leader:

Give each student a banana and ask him to give his banana a name and a personality. In addition, instruct students to write short life stories about their bananas. As a culmination activity, use markers, crayons and colored paper to create Bananart, indicating precisely what students' bananas look like in appearance (for example, happy, sad, worried, frightened). Finally, students could create graphs of all the banana faces made. Each student could hold up his banana and the class could graph whether they feel each is happy, mad, etc. Then the results could be shared aloud.

Compose a class poem entitled "Banana Appeals" (Banana Peels).

Create banana puppets, using either yellow bags or bags which can be colored yellow, by designing them after the imaginary Bananahead family. String, markers, construction paper and any other materials available will be helpful in the construction. Finally, write short banana scripts and present "bananette" (puppet) shows for the class, done entirely by the students.

Explore the encyclopedia entry for "Banana" with the class. Discuss and ask students to compile a list of at least five new things they learned from the entry.

Hide bananas around the room. Divide the class into groups. Tell each group where one of the bananas is hidden. Have that group write clues that another group can solve to help them to find the banana. Clues can be written in rhyme, humorously or very seriously.

Use the class's banana peels, after they've eaten their bananas, to create banana sculptures. Each person will attach his banana peel in an unusual way to a box weighted down with books or sand as the base. Book binding tape works marvelously to hold the peels together. Upon completion, vote on possible names for the sculptures and when they have to be dumped into the garbage, write eulogies or epitaphs and share them with the class.

As a special added treat, either at the end of your Banana Bonanza Day or during the day while students are working, hand out to students a banana, banana chips, banana nut bread, chocolate-covered bananas and/or banana-flavored candy.

GA1154

Banana Bonanza Day

Lucky Learner:

List ten new uses for banana peels.

While searching for the "perfect" banana, write an ad for the newspaper telling who, what, where, when and why this banana is so important to find.

Write a short story entitled one of the following or be creative and make up your own title:

> Monkeys Brave Cliffs for Best Bananas
> The Banana That Wore a Dress
> Bananas Boogie Back to Broadway
> One Banana, Two Banana, Three Banana, Four

Invent a new kind of superior banana and state the reason why it belongs in the Banana Hall of Fame.

Trace the shape of a banana onto a blank piece of paper. Then draw vertical and horizontal lines all the way through it. Think of five different words that describe bananas and "hide them" amongst other letters inside your banana. Exchange your secret word finds with your classmates.

Choose one of the following to write about a banana: a joke, a riddle or a tongue twister.

Compose a tall tale about "The Big Banana That Got Away!"

Write the word *bananas* vertically and think of words which describe bananas and begin with each letter.

Banana peels are often slippery if you step on them. Name as many other slippery things as possible.

Create a gameboard inside a blank file folder on which the monkey who wins gets the most bananas, and be sure to make the game rules, playing pieces, dice or spinner and any other hidden obstacles which may be encountered by the monkey on his travels.

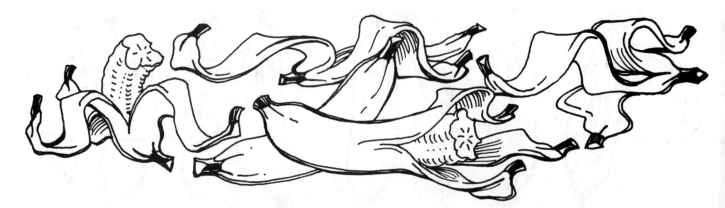

GA1154

Banana Bonanza Day

Lucky Learner:

Write five solutions to the problem of bananas spoiling so quickly just after they've been purchased.

Interview five people about bananas by posing questions like:

How would you describe the taste?

What is your most common reaction to bananas?

How is a banana like the sun?

Design an article of clothing for a banana, as if the banana were an animate object.

Mr. Bananahead has a problem. He has two weeks' vacation coming, but he can't decide where to go. Research all the places bananas are grown and then make a list of all the possible vacation spots where Mr. Bananahead might feel comfortable. Choose two or three of your favorites and share with the class.

Measure the width of one banana. Then imagine one hundred of them lined up in a row. How many total inches would that be? How many total centimeters? How many total feet?

Write a letter to the Dole Company inquiring as to why bananas come only in yellow bunches, but not in crimson clusters or polka-dotted packages or radish-red rolls or cranberry cups. Is there some reason bananas must come in bunches, or could this be changed? Offer three or four of your own suggestions.

Compile a collection of at least three desserts made with bananas and share with the class.

Compose a thriller entitled *Invasion of the Banana People* and act it out for the class.

Combine a banana, a car, a pencil and a map. What do you get? Draw it (see handout).

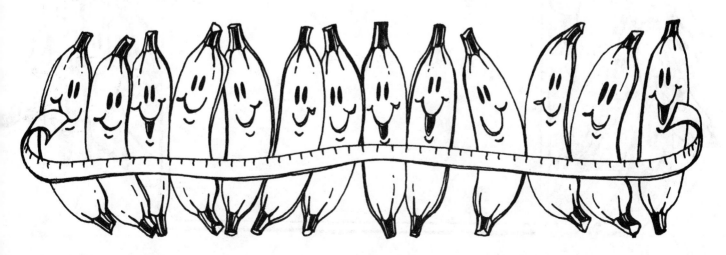

GA1154

Big Billy Bob's Banana Bonanza

Buying bananas for $1.00 a bunch brought big-eared Billy Bob and his baby brother blue-eyed Barry Boyd to the Brighton Beach Bargain Barn one brilliant blue morning. Billy Bob believed that big bright blonde bananas were better than the basic battered dull bananas that his brother Barry Boyd usually bought. So Billy Bob boasted to his mother Brenda that he could buy bountiful amounts of the best bananas this side of Broadway, and Brenda bade Billy Bob bye-bye, as he and Barry Boyd burst out of their bi-level home to battle the crowds.

At the Brighton Beach Bargain Barn, Billy Bob and Barry Boyd found the beginnings of a banana bazaar about to blast off! Billy Bob bought a dozen bunches of bright bananas, and Barry Boyd bought four bunches of not-so-bright bananas and hurried them home to Brenda. Unbeknownst to Billy Bob and Barry Boyd, they had bought the last whole bunches of bananas that the Brighton Beach Bargain Barn had to sell. Oh well!

When Billy Bob and Barry Boyd barreled in to Brenda with all those bunches of bananas, Brenda wanted to know just exactly how many bucks the boys had spent. Now if there were ten bananas in a bunch and each banana cost ten cents, how much did the boys tell Brenda the bananas had totally brought to the Brighton Beach Bargain Barn? (Simple multiplication, whole numbers)

4

GA1154

Create an Invention!

You are the famous inventor, Claude (or Claudette) Peru, and you have been given the assignment by your superior to invent the world's most incredible new contraption! However, you have only four materials with which to work and they are listed below. In some way, you are to combine these items and create something so new and unique that the world will truly be amazed! Good luck with your quest!

a banana + a car + a pencil + a map =

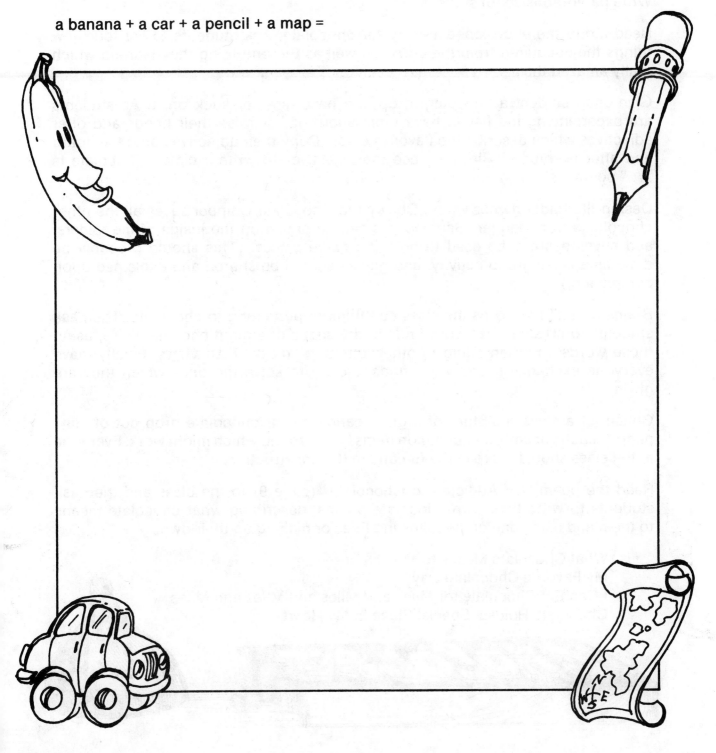

GA1154

Choco-Riffic Day

Logical Leader:

Take the class on a field trip to a local chocolate or candy-making factory or a candy store and ask factory or store employees to give a detailed description of how chocolate (candy) is made. Encourage students to ask questions.

Complete a taste test comparison between two or three of the leading candy bars. Ask students to fill out a chart, comparing the bars, using all five of their senses. Write paragraphs about students' findings.

Read aloud the encyclopedia entry for chocolate. Ask students to list four new things they acquired from the entry, as well as the one thing they learned which really amazed them.

Give each student a chocolate drop and have him/her suck on it. As students are experiencing the flavor, have them shout out or raise their hands and offer adjectives which describe the flavor in detail. Copy their adjectives onto the board and after everyone is finished, use the adjectives to write a class "Chocolate Is . . ." poem.

Design file folder games where Chewy the Chocolate Chipper saves all the other chocolates from danger. Gameboards can be drawn on the inside of file folders, and envelopes can be used to hold the game pieces. (This should probably be done as a small group activity, and games should be shared and explained upon completion.)

Brainstorm all the words the class can think of pertaining to chocolate. Then ask students to create secret word finds in the shape of a giant chocolate kiss, using those words and then filling in other letters to "mask" their views. Finally, have everyone exchange secret word finds and try to solve the ones which they are given.

Construct a class sculpture of a giant candy bar or chocolate drop out of clay, papier-mâché or any other common items lying around which might work. Everyone in the class should share in the fun and in the construction.

Read the poem "I'm Addicted to Chocolate" (page 9) to the class and then ask students to write their own chocolate poems, describing what chocolate means to them and using one of the following titles or making up their own:

What Chocolate Means to Me
My Favorite Chocolate Day
I Can Eat Chocolate for Miles and Miles and Miles and Miles
Chocolate Holds a Special Place in My Heart

Choco-Riffic Day

Lucky Learner:

Brainstorm all the foods made of or with chocolate.

Invent a new recipe in which chocolate is the main ingredient. Draw a picture of your novel concoction and actually "cook it up at home" if so desired.

Write a letter to the Hershey Company, expressing personal feelings about chocolate and its many different uses. Suggest three or four new uses for chocolate which you thought up yourself!

Write a fantasy story about the day it rained chocolate kisses.

Write three riddles about chocolate products or products made out of chocolate.

> Example: I'm short, long and flat and have lots of chocolate in me. I'm sometimes also made with peanut butter, nuts, raisins and/or cereal. I'm a quick snack with lots of sugar. What am I? (a chocolate bar)

There are many different kinds of kisses, not the least of which is the Hershey's kiss. Imagine one of those kisses to be five stories tall, a mile long, and it can talk! What will it say, where will it go and what will it do?

Name all the different ways in which chocolate can be used.

The heaviest chocolate Easter egg ever made was one weighing 7561 pounds, 13½ ounces, and measured 10 feet high! Write a story about a group of giants who hide Easter eggs this size.

Think of five favorite candy bars (chocolate, of course). Using either their whole wrappers or just part of their labels, design either a chocolate collage or a drawing which synthesizes all five.

Design chocolate note writing paper by sticking your thumb into chocolate and making chocolate thumbprint designs around the stationery. Add details with permanent ink.

7

GA1154

Choco-Riffic Day

Lucky Learner:

Create a chocolate cartoon where Charlie the Chocolate Kiss is wild about Chocolette the Chocolate Chip and wants to take her to the Three Musketeers dance.

Write a news article about the greatest chocolate story ever told! Who is involved? Why is the news scoop so great? How does it end?

Make a list of all or most of the candy bars on the market today. (This can be done by visiting a store which has a large candy department.) Categorize the candy into groups. (Example: Those with raisins, nuts, cereal, etc.) Then write Chocolate bars can be . . . vertically, and use each letter to begin either the name of an existing candy bar or some property of chocolate.

Write a science fiction story about "The Day Chocolate Took over the Earth."

Give a speech to the class about the benefits or harmful effects which the consumption of chocolate might bring about, or hold a debate where the two sides take opposing views.

Compose a play about Marvin the Mars bar, Sammy the Snickers, Arnold the Almond Joy, Melinda the Milky Way and Helen Hersheys out to battle the bad guys, Sneedly Sugar and Demon Decay, for truth and justice and the Chocolate Way!

Take the wrapper of your favorite candy bar and redesign it to make it more appealing to kids.

GA1154

I'm Addicted to Chocolate

by Lisa Rogulic-Newsome

All of my life,
Both my parents have felt . . .
That I should stay thin,
You know—skinny and svelte!

The cottage cheese, the lettuce,
And all that other diet food . . .
The yogurt, carrot sticks and celery,
Never put me in the right mood!

But no matter how very awfully low I sank,
Somehow I always came crawling right back.
I'd pick myself up and head for the kitchen,
And indulge in a gigantic milk chocolate attack!

I'd gobble down chocolate milk shakes,
Five hundred at a time.
I'd slurp acres of chocolate pudding,
So fast it was a crime!

I'd inhale chocolate chips,
Without coming up for air.
I'd eat whole chocolate pies;
I never seemed to care!

Hot chocolate I laid
By my bed late at night.
Chocolate milk for brunch
Was a choco-riffic delight!

Chocolate mousse was left for Fridays;
On Saturdays, ten or twenty floats.
I adored those hot fudge sundaes,
That came in little boats.

Finally, I certainly can't forget,
All the thousands of candy bars . . .
The Snickers, Almond Joys, Twix,
Three Musketeers and Mars!

You ask when will it all end?
Well, I really couldn't say . . .
'Cause as long as I'm alive,
These chocolate blues won't go away!

GA1154

A Wrapper of a Problem

You have been given the difficult problem of designing a candy bar wrapper which will appeal to kids of all ages and in all pangs of hunger. Neatness is important, so don't get any chocolate smudges on your paper! Color and details are also important, so don't try to hurry and get this done before the next candy bar is invented! Good luck and may the force of chocolate be with you!

GA1154

Circus Capers Day

Logical Leader:

Create a class caravan of circus wagons by directing each student to design his own wagon, with some kind of circus act going on inside. Students can use toilet paper rolls for wheels and shoe boxes for the wagons themselves. Acts can be made from clay or papier-mâché. Upon completion, attach all the wagons in a circle around the room and let the fun begin!

Read "Cloony the Clown" in Shel Silverstein's *A Light in the Attic*. Ask students to list at least ten things, besides Cloony, which are not funny.

Create circus puppets out of old socks, thread, buttons and material. Write short scripts and present mini skits about life in the circus.

Invite a circus or ex-circus performer into the classroom to share his/her experiences while under the Big Top.

Currently on the market are little packets of capsules which when submerged in water, dissolve and circus performers and scenes appear. A great science observation experiment might be for students to watch the entire dissolving process from beginning to end, jotting down just exactly what they see. Discuss the observations and see if any similarities or differences can be found.

Design a class mobile of circus performers and their individual acts. Students may work in small groups or individually for this activity. Index cards work well on which to draw the circus creations, and fish line works equally well on which to hang the cards.

Paint a huge class mural which depicts a day under the Big Top. Butcher paper may be used for the mural, and individual acts may be drawn first on construction paper and then glued on, or they may be painted directly onto the butcher paper. Give the entire mural a name by brainstorming possible choices and then voting on the best one.

Ask students to use clay to create circus animals and incorporate them into a giant class circus menagerie.

GA1154

Circus Capers Day

Lucky Learner:

Design a diorama of a three-ring circus out of a shoe box. Be as daring as possible in showing off the different acts. Use lots of variation to really make your diorama look three-dimensional.

Write a letter to Ringling Brothers-Barnum and Bailey Circus, asking them to send you the qualifications for the lion tamer's job, as they are losing the lion tamer they've had for years. Share your drafted letter and their response with the class.

Compose five riddles about circus performers and their acts. Example: I love to hang upside down and swing. What am I? (a trapeze artist).

Develop an advertising jingle for the Felix and Sons Circus, which will be coming to town in a few weeks. When will it be here? How long will it stay? How much does the circus cost? Why would anyone want to come?

Unicycles are widely ridden in circuses across the country. Bicycles and tricycles are also popular as forms of exercise and recreational fun. Make a list of all the other vehicles you can think of which also have wheels.

The circus is coming to town, and the main attraction is a new and original animal act which has never been attempted before, called . . . . Now finish the story!

Make a list of do's and don't's for a lion tamer, both humorous and serious.

Develop a fantasy story about how circuses first came to be.

Invent a new circus act and either perform or explain it to the class.

Imagine that you are the "Human Cannonball!" Just this once, while being shot out, you can travel to anywhere in the world that you'd like to go. Where would you choose to go, but more importantly, how would you get back to the circus?

GA1154

Circus Capers Day

Lucky Learner:

Which is more daring, a circus high wire act without a net or being shot out of a cannon? Brainstorm at least twenty other daring things.

How many words begin with the same letter as *circus* and also relate to the circus in some way? Make a list. (Example: cannonball)

Create five book titles which are just about to hit the best-seller list and also just happen to be about circuses.

What would happen if, all of a sudden, there were no more circuses? Who would be affected the most, adults or children? Why? Write a short paper explaining your viewpoint.

All Big Top tents are decorated in many different colors and patterns. Design an original tent cover on paper and be sure to make it bright and colorful! Or really create a tent top out of fabric and string!

Do you think that when a lion tamer puts his head inside the lion's mouth that the lion has bad breath? List some other possible pitfalls to being in the circus.

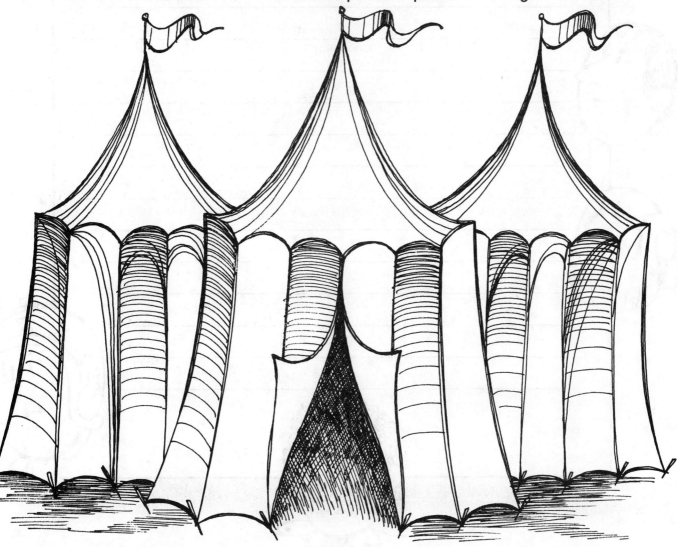

GA1154

A Mysterious Circus Situation

A trapeze artist, a human cannonball, a unicyclist, a clown and a bearded man all got caught with their hands in the cookie jar one night right before show time. A mystery unfolded. A finger could not quite be pointed at any of the five who might have left a suspicious door key in the cookie jar as each swiped his cookie.

Lots of questioning took place, but still no culprit could be discovered. Write a very suspenseful mystery centering around these five suspects, and give your ending a real BANG!

_____
_____
_____
_____
_____
_____
_____
_____
_____
_____
_____
_____
_____
_____
_____
_____

GA1154

Circus Circumstances

At a civil city in Connecticut, a circuit of circuses was claiming fame as they circulated the cleverest, craftiest and cleanest circuses ever seen. Certainly certain citizens in Carlton had passed out flyers to encourage crowds to come to their special circus, but it was uncertain as to whether the crowds would actually come.

So in order to make certain that crews of citizens would attend their circus on that clear September day, the town cinema showed a huge advertisement before every show.

It was costly, but the cinema customers chattered clear down the corridor, and many corresponded that they would certainly come to the circus that September.

It was safe to assume that several, if not hundreds or even thousands of Carlton citizens, would make it to the circus, since there were ten cinema shows a day, seven days a week, for eight weeks before the September circus date, as well as one hundred and seventy-five individuals who attended each show and saw the circus advertisement.

Now, if every single citizen who went to the cinema also attended the circus, how many total Carlton citizens enjoyed the Big Top? (Three-digit multiplication, whole numbers)

Color My World Wednesday

Logical Leader:

Read "Colors" in Shel Silverstein's *Where the Sidewalk Ends*. Ask students to write poems which incorporate as many of their favorite colors as possible.

Compose a "Color My World" class song.

Give the class a list of colors (page 19) and ask them to write color stories, using one of these titles or making up ones of their own:

> Red Roses for Rene
> The Blackest Night Ever
> Oodles of Eyes Were Green with Envy
> Blue Skies, Winking at Me
> Orange Orangutans Move In
> Yellow Yolks on You!

Ask students to write short essays stating all the different ways colors play a part in their lives, and then what life would be like if there were no color—only black and white.

Create a colorful class mobile which displays all the colors of the complete rainbow.

Ask each student to bring in a color picture which is in some way meaningful to him or her. Use the pictures to make a colorful collage and write a class poem in which every student dedicates one line.

Locate a color-blind individual and ask him to come in and speak about his handicap and how it affects his everyday life.

Examine some of the great artistic masterpieces and how color was used. Hold a class discussion about how one artist used color versus another artist and his usage. Do students feel there was a reason for their artistic choices?

Invite an artist (local or otherwise) to share his/her expertise on color with the class.

Brainstorm with the class all the "other" names they'd give to the common colors: blue, green, yellow, orange, red and purple. Then use the created color names to write name poems. Example: blue = solitude

Seatone
Off black
Loneliness
Indigo
Turquoise
Uniformed
Dazzled
Empress jewel

GA115

Color My World Wednesday

Lucky Learner:

Make nine lists, one for each of the colors (red, orange, yellow, blue, green, purple, brown, black and white), naming all those things in your world which contain each color entirely.

Design your very own color wheel.

Invent exotic new colors for tennis shoes, Legos, hair and bubble gum.

Design the world's most spectacular rainbow, unlike any ever seen before. Use material, felt, markers, crayons, colored pencils and any other colorful things you have at your disposal.

Which colors are associated with each of the holidays? Invent your own special day with one overwhelming theme color.

Write three-color "Who am I?" riddles. Share them with classmates.

Create a unique children's coloring book by which a younger child would truly be fascinated.

You have just discovered a pot of gold at the end of the rainbow. What do you do? Write a colorful story with a surprise ending.

Compose your own collection of poems about colors. Compile them into a book you make yourself.

List all the words you can think of to describe how a rainbow looks, feels, tastes and sounds.

Make up your very own color song entitled "I'm Seeing Colors Before My Eyes."

Research the most colorful animals in the world. After you've found at least ten, draw your favorite one in full color.

Write a letter to the Rainbow Maker asking him how colors are made, how they came to be and telling him how important colors are to you.

Rudolph Colorfast was a very colorful character indeed, and he sold rainbow wind chimes for a living. However, one fall day, when Rudolph went out to check his chimes, he discovered that all the blue ones were gone! Now you finish the story.

Think of something colorful which comes in a box. Now think of something colorful which can fly. Next think of something colorful which makes a lot of noise. Finally think of something colorful which stays cold most of the time. Combine these four things and what do you get? Give it a name and write an advertising jingle for it.

17

Color My World Wednesday

Lucky Learner:

Create a yellow collage and write a limerick about it. Find two words that rhyme with the word *yellow*.

Design an announcement for the birth of a Red Devil, Red Hots or Red Rover.

Make up a funny phrase about purple things, with Violet as the main character.

Write ten party tips for a gala affair, centering around the color orange.

    Example: Little orange invitations with orange candies attached should be mailed to each of the guests.

List five fears that might be associated with the color green.

Finish this story beginning "I couldn't get all my homework done! I'm soooo blue!"

Invent an original recipe for a new kind of hot fudge (brown) sundae.

Write and act out a play about the "Wonderful World of Yellow."

Use different shades of red crayons over different textures to create a "feel" picture.

Design a purple book jacket for a book about lavender items, both real and fantasy.

Create an orange greeting card to a sick person in the hospital who is badly in need of some orange juice.

Make up a daily diet that consists of only green foods.

Design a picture maze, where Bluebeard encounters various blue items along the way and ends up at the Blue Lagoon.

State five major differences between a Brownie and Girl Scout or a brownie and a cupcake.

GA115

A Rainbow of Colors

Black   ebony, raven, coal, sooty, obsidian, jet, melanoid, sable

White   snow, ivory, alabaster, bleach, blanch, milk, chalky, pale, cream, fleecy, argentine

Blue   aquamarine, baby, beryl, cobalt, eggshell blue, glaucous blue, marine, peacock, sea blue, turquoise, damson, indigo, midnight, periwinkle, wisteria, azure, navy, sapphire, cornflower, sky blue, cadet blue, ultra blue, violet-blue, blue grey, blue-green, green-blue

Red   crimson, ruby, scarlet, vermillion, cardinal, minium, carmine, cherry, wine, murrey, maroon, terra cotta, copper, puce, blush, rose, coral, mulberry, brick red, magenta, red-violet, violet-red, ultra red

Yellow   blond, lemon, sulphur, brimstone, citrus, topaz, buff, canary, chrome, primrose, apricot, flaxen, meline, luteous, fulvescent, gold, goldenrod, maise, orange-yellow, ultra yellow, grapefruit

Pink   hot magenta, carnation, salmon, ultra pink, flesh-colored, rosy, incarnadine, coral, fuchsia

Orange   peach, apricot, tangerine, burnt orange, orange-red, red-orange, melon, yellow-orange, ultra orange

Brown   amber, cafe au lait, chocolate, cocoa, coffee, dun, fawn, puce, tawny, topaz, umber, bister, ocher, raw umber, sepia, raw sienna, Indian red, tan, mahogany, bittersweet, burnt sienna

Tan   beige, biscuit, brindle, ecru, khaki

Purple   orchid, lavender, violet, thistle, blue-violet, plum, gridelin, amethyst, damson, lilac, lilaceous, mulberry, heliotrope, mauve, violaceous, perse, magenta, solferino

Green   olive, pine, green-yellow, spring green, yellow-green, sea green, forest green, ultra green, apple, boa, chartreuse, emerald, fir, jade, mignonette, pea green, peacock green, verdet, myrtle, Nile green, shamrock

GA1154

Seeing the USA in a Colorful Way

Little Rainbow Sky, along with her family, Orangette, Mellow Yellow, Red Rover, Purpletoe and Green Light had decided to take an extensive trip in their Skymobile and see the USA!

Since they lived in Whitemarsh, Pennsylvania, they started from there and the first stop was Greenville, Delaware, where the shamrocks grew out of the youngsters' ears and oodles of four-leafed clovers replaced the hair on their heads. The Skys rested there for two days.

From Greenville, the Skys went on to Orangeburg, South Carolina, where they were very surprised to see orange juice stands lining the streets and giant oranges on top of the townspeople's automobiles.

Filled with orange juice after three days, the Skys decided to plunge on to the hot chocolate capital of the world, Cocoa Beach, Florida. They found huge mugs of hot cocoa with a ton of melted marshmallows on top for everyone. After resting three days in Cocoa Beach, onward they went, this time to Blue Mound, Texas. They were truly amazed as they saw that everyone in Blue Mound had a large blue mound of bubble gum hanging off of his chin! They decided to hang out in Blue Mound for a week.

Finally rested and ready to go on, the Skys' next stop was Silver City, New Mexico. It was truly wonderful to see that everyone had silver teeth and that every time someone talked, a silver coin fell from his or her lips! The Skys stayed at Silver City only one day, and then it was time to go on to Redwood City, California. There the fun consisted of red pieces of wood making up the majority of the appliances: telephones, tape recorders, refrigerators, etc. Chief Redwood was the disc jockey on the local rock and roll station. The Skys decided to cut their trip short and spend only a day and a half in Redwood City and then head on home.

The final trip from California back to Pennsylvania took eight days, since the Skymobile broke down twice.

Now the first question is pretty easy. Just exactly how many total days did it take the Skys to travel back and forth across the USA? And lastly, if you dare, using your United States road atlas, figure out the approximate mileage the Skymobile traveled if the Skys took exactly the same route from coast to coast and then back again.

GA115

Daffy Dinosaurus Day

Logical Leader:

Read "If I Had a Brontosaurus" in Shel Silverstein's *Where the Sidewalk Ends*. Ask all the students to imagine that they each have a pet dinosaur of their own choice at home. Ask them to write poems about what they'd do with their dinosaurs and how they would care for them as they grew up.

Have the class create dinosaur puppets out of brown paper bags, yarn and markers. Ask students to write short scripts and present mini dino shows for the class.

Visit a museum of natural history or invite a historian or archaeologist into your classroom to share with the class some background or interesting information about dinosaurs.

Rent some video tapes on dinosaurs and preview them with your class, and then ask students to write movie reviews about what they've seen.

Paint a large class mural depicting numerous different dinosaurs as big and as bright as possible. Murals can represent the different groups of dinosaurs which roamed the earth at the various prehistoric times or can just show a varied range of dinosaurs drawn by the students. Then hang the completed mural on the classroom wall.

Complete the mental imagery exercise on dinosaurs in the book *200 Ways of Using Mental Imagery in the Classroom*.

Construct a huge class dinosaur diorama, where students are in charge of creating the clay dinosaurs, the background and the setting. A giant box can be cut apart on which to build the prehistoric scene. Visit a local park to collect sticks and other items from nature with which to "authenticate" the scene.

GA1154

Daffy Dinosaurus Day

Lucky Learner:

The allosaurus was nicknamed "Leaping Lizard" because of the way it lunged at its prey. *Brontosaurus* meant "Thunder Lizard" due to the fact that it was one of the largest four-legged animals which ever existed. See if you can find out what the following names meant and then give each dinosaur your own nickname: tyrannosaurus rex, brachiosaurus, pteranodon, stegosaurus, trachodon, elasmosaurus, iguanodon, anklyosaurus and triceratops.

Cross a dinosaur with a poodle and what do you get? Draw a picture of it! Now cross a dinosaur with the following things and sketch or paint a picture of each new dino-thing: sheep, can opener, car, house, pencil and flower.

Everyone has seen pictures of the outsides of many different dinosaurs. The task here is to try to imagine what the inside of a dinosaur must have been like and then draw it. What kinds of organs did a dinosaur have? Did they have blood, and if so, what did it look like? Ask yourself questions like these to get the diagram as detailed as possible, and remember to label all the parts!

If you were a dinosaur, what would you have looked like and what would your habits have been? Draw a picture of yourself, you gorgeous dinosaur, and write a paragraph about the real you!

Think about the three syllables in the word *dinosaur*. Try to come up with as many words as possible which rhyme with each syllable and list them in three columns.

Dinosaur spelled backwards is *ruasonid*, an unusual kind of plant only in Ruasonia. (Ha! Ha!) Take the names of at least ten different dinosaurs and write them backwards. (Make sure you have the spellings correct to begin with!) Then invent definitions for the new words.

Invent five titles for songs about dinosaurs.

Design a dinosaur-making machine which makes the largest of dinosaurs, and even the smallest of children can figure out how it works!

GA11

Daffy Dinosaurus Day

Lucky Learner:

A giant tyrannosaurus rex was coming right at me! I didn't have my weapon at my side, so I . . . . Now finish the story!

Write an advice column answering questions about problems which might have occurred if dinosaurs still roamed the world today. One possible question you might be asked would be, "If dinosaurs were alive today, just where would they be living?" The questions could come from your classmates or you could make them up yourself.

There are numerous theories explaining why dinosaurs became extinct. Portray any personal beliefs you might have on this matter in a brief one-page essay.

Create a science fiction story where dinosaurs have supernatural powers and are using them for the betterment of mankind.

Imagine having to use only dinosaurs as a means of transportation. Write an eight-line humorous poem describing what it might be like.

Brainstorm and make a list of as many different dinosaurs as possible.

Vertically write the words *delving into dinosaurs*. With each letter, begin a word that describes (adjective) a specific dinosaur or dinosaurs in general. Or you could use the letters to begin the names of many different kinds of dinosaurs, too.

Think of five of your favorite dinosaurs. Now think of one characteristic from each which you admire. Synthesize those five characteristics into one brand-new, never-been-thought-of-before dinosaur! Give it a name and describe its eating, mating, sleeping and protecting habits in a descriptive paragraph.

If someone could create the "ideal" dinosaur, what qualities or features might he or she add to those dinosaurs which existed to create the very best dinosaur ever? Make a list.

GA1154

Dinosaur Dreaming

Below are presented to you several different situation statements, which you are to ponder for a few minutes and then answer with one or two paragraphs in essay form. Have fun with them!

You have been accused of stealing a pteranodon from the local zoo. What are you going to do?

Someone left a baby tyrannosaurus rex in your front yard in a blue basket. What will you do?

While fishing in the local ponds, you snagged an ichthyosaurus on its way out. What do you do?

You were left by your parents in a haunted house, haunted by the ghost of allosaurus. What now?

While making a tree house in your backyard, a small triceratops shows up and wants to play. Do you?

One day at school, a stegosaurus wandered in through the front door. What does your principal do?

A brachiosaurus is the rock concert's main attraction, except it can't carry a tune. What should the audience do?

All the dinosaurs returned to Earth, only this time they were gentle and kind. The problem is where and with whom should they live?

A family of ankylosauruses want to attend your church, but there's no room in the pews on Sunday. What can the pastor do?

You are lost in a very dark jungle and a brontosaurus decides to roam around. You can't escape his huge footprints and the sound of his roar, so what do you do?

GA115

Daffy's Delicious Dinner

Daily, at the Dinosaur Diner on Dillwinkle Drive, a dangerously dumb dinosaur named Daffy dampened his fifty darts in deluxe desserts of dreamy delights and downed them, dozens at a drop.

Doughnuts, five dozen, were gobbled down by Daffy before he went on to devour 121 dictionaries, 83 hot doggies and 5 diet Dr. Peppers.

But Daffy wasn't done yet! He drank 74 drums of different drinks, 4 dollups of dirt dissolved in Drano and digested 213 drowning wooden ducks, before he went out to duel a dramatic deer named Dillard.

Daffy didn't disturb the doctor, who lived a dozen doors down from the diner, or the drifter who danced for dough. Daffy did, however, get an upset tummy from digesting all of those doughnuts, desserts, dictionaries, hot doggies, diet Dr. Peppers, drums of drinks, dirt and dumb ducks.

Just exactly how many total things did Daffy drink and devour?

GA1154

Deluxe Dragon Day

Logical Leader:

After your students are totally relaxed, take them on this mental imagery exercise:

> You are a knight and a dragon slayer, wandering through the hills and dales, searching for ferocious dragons. You picked up the scent of one a while back and by the way your horse is acting, you know the dragon is near.
> You camp inside a small cave, but during the night you hear a terrible noise right outside. You arm yourself with the fire extinguisher, peer out, but when you see the dragon, you can't believe your eyes!

Now ask your students to draw a detailed picture of the dragon they saw.

Present your class with the creative dramatics activities on dragons in the book *Secrets & Surprises* by Joe Wayman and Lorraine Plum (Carthage, IL: Good Apple, Inc, 1977).

Create dragons out of magazine advertisements. Allow students time to cut out five advertisements each. Then ask students to determine which ad will constitute the dragon's head, body, legs and arms, tail and eyes. Next, ask them to trade body parts with classmates so that they end up with a totally different set of dragon parts. Ask students to create a dragon using the five "body parts" they are holding by gluing them collectively together onto a piece of white paper. They may add features with markers, crayons and colored pencils. Finally, encourage students to name their dragons and write funny stories about how they came to be.

Read "Dragon of Grindly Grun" in Shel Silverstein's *A Light in the Attic*. Have students pretend that they too are dragons and ask them to describe their eating habits in an eight-line humorous poem.

Cut out different pieces of poster paper the lengths of your students and give each student his or her own piece. Ask each student to place the paper flat on the floor and have a partner do the same. Then ask one partner to lie down on the paper and curl up into the most ferocious dragon shape he possibly can, while you instruct the other partner to trace his shape onto the paper. The two partners then switch roles until two dragons are completely drawn. Next the dragons are cut out and decorated with odds and ends of fabric, markers, feathers, etc. Finally, the dragons' life stories are told, either orally or on paper. These life-size dragons can help decorate the room for Chinese New Year as well!

GA1154

Deluxe Dragon Day

Lucky Learner:

How many different ways could dragons help us if only they were real? Make a list.

Take the words *dragons don't cry*. Make as many names of dragons as possible out of the letters, in any arrangement, from those three words. (Example: Yogar the stepbrother to Togar the Dragon)

How could someone help an elderly dragon who could no longer breathe fire? Write down at least five options he might have.

What if it was found that a dragon was living in your best friend's backyard, right under the tree house? What are some of the things which might be done?

How do dragons learn to terrorize kingdoms, kidnap fair maidens and virtually become the "bad guys"? Why shouldn't dragons be the "good guys," out to help the kingdoms and save the damsels in distress? Design a Learner's Manual for the Proper School of Etiquette for Dragons and Dragonettes, listing at least five proper manners a sophisticated dragon should have.

Prepare a menu which dragons might like if knights and fair maidens were scarce.

Having just met a very nice dragon who likes people and who is trying to find a job in the open market, make a job wanted ad for the dragon, as well as include at least three jobs for which he might be qualified.

Compose a song entitled "My Best Friend Is a Dragon!"

GA1154

Deluxe Dragon Day

Lucky Learner:

If a dragon could talk, what might it say? Write a make-believe conversation which might occur between a dragon and a dragonfly.

Cross a dragon with a Siamese cat and what do you get? What about a cross between a dragon and a doctor? Choose one of these two combinations and write about the newly created creature's plight to try to fit in with a "normal" population.

If one thing could be done to improve a dragon, what would it be and why?

Make a list of all the adjectives which could be used to describe dragons. Then write the word *dragon* vertically and use the letters to begin different dragon describers.

Invent a dragon-catcher mobile which would aid dragon catchers in their quest for escaped dragons (see handout).

What does a dragon smell like? Sound like? Taste like? Feel like? Use your senses to imagine the answers to these questions.

If you were a dragon, what would your name be? What would you look like? What would be your quest?

What could someone do with a dragon besides capture it? Make a list.

GA1154

Catch 'Em While You Can!

The quaint town of Dragonville is in desperate need of a dragon-catcher mobile! Dragonville's dragon slayer, Dapper Danton Delbert, can then go out into the thick, deep forests and catch the devilish dragons, place them into the dragon-catcher mobile and transport them into the faraway land of Dragon Heights, a retirement community for dragons. There they can live out their remaining years in comfort, without any possible opportunity to harm damsels or dragon slayers ever again.

Your job is to create this dragon-catcher mobile, with every modern convenience and detail known to mankind. Make sure to label all the parts so others will understand just exactly how your massive machine really works!

GA1154

Dragonalogies

Analogies are really just comparisons between one similarity or opposite idea and another. Once you understand the first part of an analogy, then the second part should reveal itself and become easy to complete. Create answers for the following analogies which are given, and keep in mind that in several analogies more than one answer is possible. Good luck!

Dragon slayer is to dragon as dogcatcher is to _____

Five dragons are to ten dragons as fifteen dragons are to _____

Fire is to dragons as _____ is to elephants.

Vice Presidents are to Presidents as knights are to _____

A forest is to a dragon as an ocean is to a _____

Gentle is to ferocious as a fair maiden is to a _____

A mouse is to a dragon as an ant is to an _____

A dragon's tail is to a dragon as a _____ is to a knight.

A den is to a _____ as a teepee is to an Indian.

The dragon-catcher mobile is to a dragon as a police car is to a _____

GA1154

Eggciting Eggtivities Day

Logical Leader:

Hand out two hard-boiled eggs to each student, one for eating and one with which to work. Ask students to name their individual eggs and write physical descriptions of them on paper.

Compose an "Ode to an Egg" while working in small groups. Share with the class.

Decorate eggs with markers. Prepare and present "eggpet" (puppet) shows for everyone.

Read the encyclopedia entry for eggs. Discuss the different parts of an egg, and have students draw detailed diagrams of the inside of a large egg.

Draw a picture of a huge egg on the chalkboard or on a large sheet of poster paper. Brainstorm with the class all the words that could in any way relate to an egg. Then use the brainstormed vocabulary to write an "eggy" class collection of riddles.

Throughout the Eggtivity Day, share with the class samples of egg drop soup, egg salad sandwiches, deviled eggs and an assortment of candy Easter eggs.

Eggciting Eggtivities Day

Lucky Learner:

Talk to the egg, either orally or on paper, and say everything creative one could possibly say to an egg, like "The yolks on you!" or "You crack me up!"

Create eggwriting stories, using one of these titles or by making up a creative title of your own:

  Eggs Conquer the Pots and Pans
  King Eggward and Queen Eggsmerelda Get Egged
  Eggs Get Eggsactly What They Deserve
  Eggsters Have Eggvantage Over Eggheads

Make a list of all the foods into which eggs can become a part.

Compose a song entitled "You Egg Up My Life!"

Invent four new uses for eggs and their shells.

Write a script for a show which centers around six eggheads.

Compose individual "Ballad of the Egg" tunes.

List five reasons why eggs are healthy and good for you.

Transcribe seven short letters to familiar people, eggnonimously.

GA1154

Eggciting Eggtivities Day

Lucky Learner:

Brainstorm at least eight eggcellent topics about which it would be fun to learn more about and make a list.

In your own words, write seven reasons why an egg is colored brown or white and not pink or purple.

Write five yolks (jokes) about eggs!

List three food dishes which can be made from eggplant.

Write a conversation which might occur between Eggbert and Eggward.

"As I walked into the grocery store, I couldn't believe my eyes! There, everywhere— on the cereal, in the frozen food section, behind the baked goods, under the meat— were rows and rows of eggs! Small ones, medium ones, large ones and even extra large eggs—EVERYWHERE, dozens and dozens of eggs! They had planned a massive takeover of the store, and I was to play a major role in their scheme." Now really finish the story!

Eggsactly eighty-eight eggs egged eggheads every eighty-eight days. Now write an original tongue twister about eggs!

GA1154

Eggspecially Eggciting Eggs

Every Easter, eight hundred and eighty-eight eggcited eggs have entered Eggland and egged King Eggsmond and Queen Eggsmerelda. Eventually, of course, Eggsmond and Eggsmerelda elected to live elsewhere, but it took eighty-eight years for this to happen. With this in mind, how many eggsotic Easter eggs have egged Eggsmond and Eggsmerelda over the years?

Eggsamine another scenario. Eggsmond and Eggsmerelda purchased eggcellent Easter eggs of their own, at the rate of twenty dozen eggsactly every year, to diseggcourage and egg-off the other eggcited Easter eggs. Each felt it eggually necessary to try to defend their elevated honor. Eggscaping none, eggstablish how many total eggs Eggsmond and Eggsmerelda bought over the last eighty-eight years.

If Eggsmond was six years old when he first came to Eggland and Eggsmerelda was eight, how old were they by the time they left? (Addition, two and three-digit multiplication, whole numbers)

GA1154

Fantastic Fire Friday

Logical Leader:

Visit the local fire station or invite a fireman into the classroom to teach the class about fire safety and prevention.

Construct a class mobile with pictures of "various fires just waiting to happen." Ask students to draw possible accident sites to help caution others.

Invite a Boy Scout into the classroom to share with the students the methods of starting a fire without matches.

Ask a chimney sweep or person knowledgeable in this area to come and offer his expertise about fireplaces and their care.

Take the class on a fantasy trip to the fun world of flame and fortune! Brainstorm all the different places in the world where fire is the catalyst in making some kind of fun occur. Then incorporate those into a mental imagery exercise, during which time students can relax, shut their eyes and imagine they are at the various scenes brainstormed earlier and use all their senses to smell, hear, taste, see and feel and do all there is to do. (Examples of possible scenes include Fourth of July fireworks, a camping bonfire, a forest fire, etc.)

Ask students to imagine that their homes have been totally destroyed by fire and burned to the ground. Encourage them to make a list of the ten most important items they had in their houses prior to the fire which they would have saved, given the chance. Compare and contrast students' lists.

Compose a class ballad entitled "Fire Can Kill," warning others of the hazards of playing with matches.

Design a class flag in honor of all the good that fire does.

Create greeting cards where the greeting itself should have something to do with fire. (Example: You light up my life.)

GA1154

Fantastic Fire Friday

Lucky Learner:

Name all the words or phrases which come to mind when the word *fire* is mentioned.

The Fire God was very real to many ancient civilizations as it even is to some now. Write a myth with your very own Fire God (see handout).

Imagine that someone was in a house which had started on fire. If the doors were all blocked, what would be some options for escape?

Having just been "fired" from a job for something which wasn't anyone's fault, list all of the things which might be done to try to get the job back.

List ten things over which someone could really get "fired" up!

In an adventure story, the hero is about to be shot by a firing squad. But right at the last minute, right after "Ready . . . Aim . . ." something truly miraculous happens! Create an original "Our Hero Saves the Day" adventure story.

There is an old saying "Fight fire with fire." Write a paragraph or two discussing what this paragraph means.

Someone set fire to the "fireworks" company down the street. The only clues to the culprit are an old lighter monogrammed with the letter *C*, a dirty handkerchief with one very noticeable fingerprint and a pair of broken eyeglasses. As the fireworks are going off in the distance, solve the crime!

Smokey the Bear says, "Only you can prevent forest fires." Make up twenty rules which everyone should follow to accomplish this feat.

Fantastic Fire Friday

Lucky Learner:

Create a scenario (story) which includes a fireball (candy), a fire hydrant and a fire extinguisher which takes place at least part of the time in a fire station.

If you were a flame, where would you go? What would you do that would benefit others?

Make a list of all the different uses for fire you can brainstorm.

Create a recipe for flame pudding, using either realistic or imaginary ingredients.

Design a diorama out of a shoe box which depicts a fire infiltrating some type of building.

Finish this phrase in at least ten different ways:

     Fire is as hot as . . .

What are the sights, sounds, smells, tastes and feelings at the scene of a fire?

Design a fire truck of the future. Either illustrate it or build an actual model.

How is fire similar to an angry temper? How is fire different from a hot electric stove? Write complete paragraph answers.

What if fire suddenly were cold? What alternative(s) to fire do we have for cooking? For heating? For igniting fireworks and bonfires?

GA1154

Fire, a Magical Myth

The Greeks and the Romans often wrote myths, which were traditional stories of historical events that often explained a practice, belief or natural phenomenon.

You are about to write your own myth which will explain the phenomenon of fire. You can create your own Fire God or present your imaginary story in another way. Just make sure you use everything you know about fire to write your myth and make it as wonderfully clever as possible! Good luck in your enterprise! FIRE UP!

38

A Friday Fire Festival

Five Fridays ago, a fire festival was held to familiarize families with fire safety and prevention. First, four seminars were given helping folks to face the problem of fires in the front foyers of their homes. Next, a fair amount of fastening and loosening of fire suits was done to make folks fashion conscious in regard to fire attire.

A fair amount of fear was instilled by a film which featured a fierce fire overtaking a five-star restaurant in Freeport. Fellows began to fidget and pointed their fingers at the use of cigars and cigarettes. But who can figure out the cause for sure?

A finale to the festivities included a friendly fireman named Fred who made an unbelievable find at the fiesta table of fine food. Before Fred had finished, he'd filled his tummy full of 110 frankfurters, 57 frijoles, 462 fritos, 54 fig newtons, 27 fudgcicles, 19 pieces of the finest fudge, 309 apple fritters, a fat piece of flounder and 639 French fries, not to mention the five dozen floats he drank!

As the crowd was leaving, Fred the fireman asked, "Just exactly how many total foods did I eat and drink?" Can you help him out?

Garbage Gazing Day

Logical Leader:

Prior to this day, assign students to list at least twenty-four pieces of garbage in their home garbage pails, and ask students to bring their lists to class on Garbage Gazing Day. In addition to the list, students are also to bring to class four pieces of nonperishable trash for use on the sculpture. When the day arrives, give each student four, three-inch pieces of book binding tape which they'll need to roll in order to make it sticky on all four sides. Students will have to use one piece of tape per garbage piece. When it's time to assemble the sculpture, each student will select one of his pieces of garbage, line up and place it somewhere onto a large piece of thick cardboard or poster board. The next student attaches his garbage to his classmate's in some obscure way until all of the pieces of trash have been in some way attached to the sculpture. Finally, each child names the sculpture and the class votes on the best name. A culmination activity might be to have the students write art gallery descriptions of the garbage sculpture, read them aloud and see whether, from their descriptions, anyone might be interested in "purchasing" the sculpture.

Read "Sarah Cynthia Sylvia Stout Would Not Take the Garbage Out" in Shel Silverstein's *Where the Sidewalk Ends*. Then ask students to write poems in which their experiences, both real and imaginary, relate to taking the garbage out.

Invite a city sanitation employee into the classroom to explain to the students the process which occurs with the garbage after it leaves their homes until it arrives at the dump.

Using semi-flat, nonperishable garbage, create a giant class garbage collage.

Collect brochures from the various recycling agencies around town and share them with the class. They can serve as great discussion starters! Or invite someone in who has some very strong views or opinions on recycling to talk with students and to at least offer them some background information about recycling.

Create a paper garbage mobile by hanging interesting-looking garbage wrappers from a long wooden stick, the kind you can buy inexpensively from a plant store. Fish line works well for hanging.

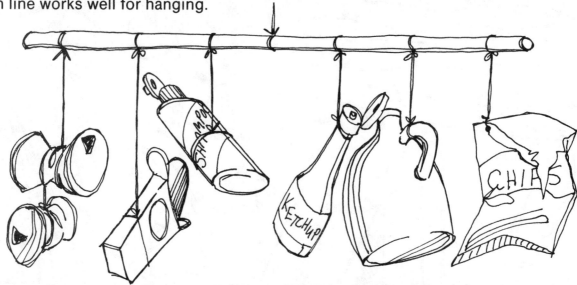

GA1154

Garbage Gazing Day

Lucky Learner:

In how many different ways can garbage help man? Make a list.

Take the names of fifteen different pieces of garbage in your pail or bucket at home, scramble the letters in each of the names to create an artistic design onto a large piece of paper and give the finished product a name.

Take any two pieces of garbage and combine them together to form a brand-new product (see handout).

Name five ways individuals could physically as well as through their support offer assistance to their local garbage company to help keep their city clean.

What would happen if the garbage company went out on strike for an entire month? What would happen to your town? What could you do personally to aid in garbage conservation?

Design the perfect garbage bag, one that is attractive enough for housewives to want to use and one that is utilitarian enough and strong enough to insure correct garbage disposal and storage.

Make up a story about Hillbilly Barney, the old hermit who locked himself up in a cabin for one hundred years and never, ever took his garbage out!

If you were a piece of garbage, what piece would you be and what kind of adventure would you have on the way to the junkyard?

Garbage Gazing Day

Lucky Learner:

Name all the words possible which begin with the same letter as *garbage*. Write a tongue twister.

What can someone do with garbage besides throw it away? Make a list.

Oscar the Grouch lives in a garbage can. Where does Grindle the Garbage Monster reside? What other garbage creatures can you create, and just exactly where do they live?

What if garbage were literally worth its weight in gold? What would change in the world?

Which is worse—not taking out your garbage for weeks or littering the street? Write a persuasive argument to back up your opinion.

Using only the letters in *take the garbage out*, how many different names of garbage can be made? (Example: rutabaga)

A giant garbage ball is rolling towards your town in a big hurry! Your family needs to evacuate your home as soon as possible. You can take only a few things with you when you go. Make a list of the ten most important things you'd want to save in case the garbage ball rolled over your house.

Create a cartoon which features Gumbo the Garbage Guru, and his plight to outlaw litter in the neighborhoods.

Design a button which encourages people not to litter by displaying some kind of witty campaign slogan.

GA1154

Garbage Creates New Products!

After looking through one's garbage, it becomes quite evident that if two pieces of garbage (or products) were combined in name, function and container, a new product could be formed which was far better than either of the original products.

Listed below are ten pairs containing two pieces of garbage each, which you are to combine into ten new items with unique names, special functions and totally new and functional containers. An example is given.

Garbage Items	New Name	Function	Container
Rice Chex + Friskies Buffet	Frisk Chex	crunchy cat food	canox (half can, half box)
Lemonade cup + old hairbrush			
TV dinner box + empty vitamin jar			
Noodles in a cup + video tape wrapper			
Fresh mushroom container + paper plate			
Olive can + ½ ice-cream cone			
Captain Crunch box + broken hammer			
Twix candy wrapper + bottle cap			
Magazine + old toothbrush			
Rolled up newspaper + empty Kleenex box			
Brownie mix box + remains of bar of soap			

GA1154

Cash for Trash?

In this nation, garbage is picked up on the average of twice a week with two pails of trash collected each time from each home. As the population increases, so does its trash. Eventually, and in some cities even now, towns are becoming so overwhelmed with trash that there may not be any place suitable enough for disposal, and that presents a major problem.

Your mission at this time is to present a variety of different solutions.

First, devise a method to recycle the paper, plastic, glass and metal in the most desirable way, by brainstorming some possible uses for all that garbage!

Second, develop a system to sort different by-products, both in the home and in the garbage truck. Again, the best method for arriving at an idea and thus determining the ultimate solution is to brainstorm several different methods and evaluate which one would work the best.

These problems are difficult and will ultimately be facing us all, but if you put your mind to it, you can certainly generate some ideas which could be the answers to our problems! Good luck!

GA1154

Heroic Heroes Day

Logical Leader:

Invite a local hero into the classroom. Ask the class to prepare interview questions prior to his or her visit. When the visitor has left, ask the class to evaluate just exactly what made this individual a hero and specifically in whose eyes.

Have the students create puppets which resemble their favorite heroes. Then ask them to put on mini puppet shows for their class.

View a videotape which depicts a modern hero (Batman, Rocky, Karate Kid, etc.). Ask students to write critical reviews and determine at least five criteria which will or will not determine whether this person is a hero, at least in the students' eyes.

Ask the class to draw their own comic book heroes, either real or imaginary, doing some heroic deeds. Then hang all of them under a large bulletin board display entitled "Our Heroes!"

Ask the class to research some of the great heroes of the past like Benjamin Franklin; Martin Luther King, Jr.; Abraham Lincoln; Charles Lindbergh; Amelia Earhart; Neil Armstrong; Thomas Edison; Thomas Jefferson; Davy Crockett; Daniel Boone and any others they may have read about in the past and found interesting. After collecting their research, compile the information into a fact file of index cards.

Have students design flags which honor their favorite heroes. Hang from the classroom ceiling.

Assign small groups to design games to commemorate their favorite heroes. Gameboards can be drawn on file folders and obstacles can include all the things a hero might have to encounter until he reaches the end of the board, where some surprise should happen. Then groups should switch games and play one another's.

Assign a different "hero" to each member of the class. Students are to research ten to twenty interesting facts about their heroes, incorporate them into brief life stories, find costumes that the heroes might wear and then present themselves as their heroes to the class.

Find pictures of famous heroes in various library books. Make sure that each student has a picture, a piece of watercolor paper and a set of watercolors. Ask students to try to paint copies of their heroes to the best of their ability.

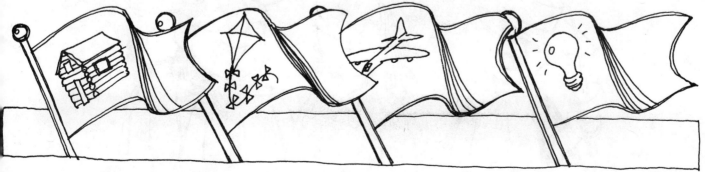

GA1154

Heroic Heroes Day

Lucky Learner:

Make a list of all the heroes, both past and modern, which have evolved out of books, TV shows and movies.

What makes a person a hero in someone's eyes? Write a short essay explaining what makes a hero to a child under ten, a teenager and an individual over eighteen years of age.

Think about some of these comic book characters: Superman, Dick Tracy and Spiderman. Why or why not would you classify these three as heroes? Make a list of pros and cons for each side. (Heroes versus Nonheroes)

Write a character sketch about the "perfect" hero and draw a picture as well. What must he do to make him great? Who has to know about his feat? How many people must be aware of what he has done? Keep these questions in mind as you mold your character.

The Lone Ranger and the Cisco Kid (and Poncho) are a few heroes from yesteryear. Zorro and Robin Hood are also TV and film stars of the past. What modern day heroes would you equate these four heroes to, and what criteria will you use? (Example: Robin Hood is like the town mayor because he taxes the wealthy and tries to give to the poor and homeless.)

Crocodile Dundee and Rambo are both making it big in the movie houses as current day heroes. What makes them so appealing? List their five main attractions to the public.

The world was at a standstill. All the buildings were burning, the people were crowding the streets, but there was nowhere to go. The Garbanoyle Monster had rampaged and demolished city after city. There was only one chance left for Dothom Town and that was . . . . Now finish the story, using the name and personality of your favorite hero.

Captain Marvel and Batman were caped crusaders who stood for truth and justice and the capture of all criminals, both big and small. Invent a caped crusader of your own who will save your school from juvenile delinquents who want to lure students into cheating on their exams and others who steal food from the cafeteria.

GA1154

Heroic Heroes Day

Lucky Learner:

Name at least ten motivations which a hero might need in order to do a good deed. (Example: If someone were to see a small child being kidnapped, a robbery in progress, etc., then he might do a good deed and, hence, become a hero.)

The Bionic Man and Bionic Woman could perform unusually heroic feats just through the use of their bodies. If you could develop a Super Person, what characteristics would he or she have to have?

There are a lot of heroes around who maybe aren't on TV or in the movies, but who nonetheless save lives. One example of these heroes might be the doctors of the world. Give eight other examples of some not-quite-so-famous heroes of this day and age.

You have just accomplished a really heroic feat! Describe what it was and how you felt after doing it!

How many different ways can you think of in which heroes help us? Make a list.

Take the letters in *Once a hero, very knowledgeable sources say, always a hero.* Brainstorm as many words as possible which either name heroes or are in some way are connected to heroes by using only the letters in those ten words. (Example: saves)

Think about any three of your favorite heroes. Take the best qualities from each one and develop a fourth and even greater hero and human being.

You have a friend who accomplished a lifesaving gesture, but now his action has given him a feeling that he can do no wrong. Write a letter to him, telling him how you feel about his actions.

Write a ten-line poem, where every line rhymes with the first:

    I once knew a full-fledged hero . . .

Everyone needs someone to look up to. Write a speech to give to young children, explaining what a hero is, who some of the heroes might be and why it is so important to have a hero to look up to for guidance and direction.

GA1154

Heroic Heroes

Half of the heroic heroes in history have helped humans out of their bad habits and hair-raising, half-baked schemes.

Consider the happening where our handsome, handy, heroic hero, Hugo Horatio Humor helped the highwaymen handle a hard case. A group of high school students were suspected of hauling off a valuable Hindu vase from the Highland Headquarters for Heavy Hearts. Hugo took a handful of fingerprints before he hastened to collect the other clues: a hammer, handkerchief and wall hanging of a hundred headlights.

Honestly, Hugo had heard that it took seven huge hunky guys to carry the Hindu vase and another twenty to lift the vase into the van. After it was safely inside, it took four hunks to hover over it for protection and finally another ten hunks to unload it and carry it away.

Hugo figured out that it took a whole gang to harmonize the execution of the theft. But there were hundreds of gangs hanging around the high school. The only way Hugo could hand the guilty gang over to the highwaymen was to determine just exactly how many hunks it took to completely heist the Hindu vase. Can you help him out? (Simple addition, whole numbers)

Heroic Heroes Are Fearless!

Use each letter below to be included in adjectives describing heroes or nouns naming popular pastimes or current day heroes in this Heroic Heroes Are Fearless name poem. (Hint: Use your thesaurus for help!)

Example:

```
      cHampion-like
bravE
   daRing
    liOnhearted
  vallant
       Courageous
```

```
H
E
R
O
I
C

H
E
R
O
E
S

A
R
E

F
E
A
R
L
E
S
S
!
```

49

GA1154

I Said It's Red Monday!

Logical Leader:

For the older kids, discuss the difference between a red communistic form of government like that in China and a red, white and blue form of democracy like the one in the United States.

Using magazines, have students design a giant collage around the theme of Red. Then write "Red is . . . ." poems about the collage.

Hand out a few red-hot candies to each student. Have them fill out a senses chart which includes how the candies taste, feel, smell, sound and look. After they have eaten the red-hots, have them describe how their mouths feel in a paragraph which begins "Eating red-hots is just like . . . ."

Use red and white paint to create at least ten different shades of red. Ask students to use the various shades to paint a mural around the theme of Radical Red.

Complete the creative dramatics activities on strawberries in the book *Secrets & Surprises* by Joe Wayman and Lorraine Plum (Carthage, IL: Good Apple, Inc., 1977).

Read the following story starter to your class:

> One early evening in October, a blood red pepper was discussing his views about those little red things that come in olives known as pimentoes. You see, the red pepper was jealous of the pimentos and wanted to do away with them. His plan was fast at work, but then something went wrong! Now you finish the story!

Hold a red cookie making party! Use the simple sugar cookie recipe below plus a little red food coloring to make the cookies. Then use all kinds of red sprinkles, red icing and red candy to decorate the tops. When you are finished, hold a contest for the best Red Zinger Cookie!

Sugar Cookie Recipe

¾ cup Crisco	1 teaspoon baking powder	1 cup sugar
1 teaspoon vanilla	1 teaspoon salt	2 eggs
2½ cups flour		

> Mix the sugar, vanilla, eggs and Crisco thoroughly. Sift flour once and blend with baking powder and salt. Cover the bowl and chill in refrigerator for two hours. Heat the oven to 400 degrees. Roll dough ⅛-inch thick and cut into various shapes that have to do with the theme of Red. Place cookies on ungreased baking sheet. Bake 5-8 minutes or until golden brown. Voila!

Ask your students to research all the animals they can which contain names with the word *red* in them. (Example: red snapper) Make a class list and discuss the specific reasons each of these animals might have been called "red this" or "red that." (Example: The red-tailed hawk has a red tail.)

50

GA1

I Said It's Red Monday!

Lucky Learner:

Red sounds like . . . Red feels like . . . Red smells like . . . Red tastes like . . . Red looks like . . . Now complete these statements!

If you could be red, what would you be? Name at least ten really different ideas!

List all the different shades and colors of red that you can think of.

Create imaginary recipes for Red Ribbon Surprise, Roast Cranberry Delight, Maroon Macaroons, Ruby Red Riddlers and Tomato Strawberry Mousse.

Name all the things which can make the color red. (Example: markers, crayons, etc.)

Design a new article of clothing in at least three different shades of red.

As I entered the classroom, all I could see was red! There were cranberry red chalkboards, mulberry red bulletin boards, ruby red desks and a giant piece of watermelon sitting right behind the teacher's desk! I thought I was dreaming, so I pinched myself, but when I looked at my arm, I realized my skin was bright red, too! How could I escape this nightmare? Now give this story an electrifying ending!

When people get embarrassed, they usually turn ten shades of red. Make a list of at least nine truly embarrassing things.

Think of your favorite musicians and paint a poster in red of that musical group.

Make a list of every red candy you can think of. Then use the names of those candies in a wildly sweet and rosy story entitled "Sweets Are 'Red' (read) Wrong by Police!"

GA1154

I Said It's Red Monday!

Lucky Learner:

List all of the names (persons, places and things) which come to mind when the color red is mentioned.

Write a conversation which might occur between a red heart and a tomato.

Compose red stories, which may be written in red ink, red crayon or red marker. Titles may include:

> Too Many Reds Spoil the Whole Bunch
> Reds Sing the Blues While They Are Green with Envy
> Oh No! Red Is Missing from the Rainbow!
> An Apple a Day Will Keep Mean Ghosts Away!

Write a newspaper article telling the real story behind "The Day Red Was Removed from Disneyland."

What would happen if someone crossed a tomato with a rose? How about crossing a cardinal with a heart? Or a radish with a pair of ruby lips? Make up as many different combinations as possible with red things and see what will happen!

Make up a list of at least ten red items. Then mix up the letters in each one's name and create the names of ten other "red" things for which you are to write the definitions. (Example: tomato = OTTOMA, a red-faced kid who says, "Ought to, Ma!" a lot!)

What would happen if all the red were removed from the world? How would things change? Write a one-page essay discussing this topic.

Ringo Red, the red fox, has escaped from the zoo and is nowhere to be found. An APB (All Points Bulletin) has been issued by the police, but you, an undercover private eye, have just been hired by the zoo to find the red fox first. You have only one clue to the red fox's whereabouts. He loves to eat small mice. Now get started on your step-by-step plan to capture Ringo Red.

Red can be smooth or it can be rough. Think of at least ten opposites to describe red and give examples for each.

GA115

Red Listing

Listing is a wonderful way to brainstorm topics and help to get you in touch with a specific area you may want to further research at a later time. Below you are given ten questions which should inspire ten "lists," and a good test would be to see if you could complete this page within ten minutes, while generating loads of ideas at the same time! Have fun!

List one red thing with which to write.

List two kinds of red flowers.

List three kinds of red vehicles.

List four red vegetables.

List five red things to wear on your head.

List six kinds of red clothing.

List seven red foods.

List eight red three-syllable words.

List nine red three-syllable words.

List nine red color words.

List ten red things you might wear on your feet.

GA1154

Rene's Red-Letter Day

Rene Randie Reddington arose one Monday morning, and to her surprise, her world had suddenly turned bright red! Everywhere Rene looked, everything was colored in shades of red, and whether Rene realized it or not, this was going to be a red-letter day!

At breakfast, Rene saw three red robins, four mulberry ravens, five blood red cardinals and a brick red raccoon.

After she finished her breakfast sitting on her rosy rattan chair, Rene put on her wrinkled scarlet red outfit and got "ready" for work. Rene looked out of the window and saw it was raining red cats and red doggies—twenty of them! Her crimson rag doll and her brother's magenta rattle were sitting on the violet-red counter. She also saw that her little brother Rudolph's railroad set and his road rally kit were also bright red.

Rene rode her Renault to Reese's Roadhouse where she played fifty-six red records, and wrote nineteen red recipes before returning home. For dinner, Rene had two plates of rare roast beef, twelve red radishes, twenty-six pieces of red ravioli and a round of ten red strawberry drinks.

Just exactly how many total red things did Rene encounter during her rosy day? (Simple addition, whole numbers)

GA11

I Scream for Ice-Cream Day!

Logical Leader:

Visit an ice-cream parlor that has a variety of flavors, or invite someone to come and speak to the class about the wide variety of ice-cream flavors and all the different uses for ice cream. In addition, ask him or her to explain how ice cream is made.

Purchase six or seven different flavors of ice cream. Blindfold students and conduct taste tests to determine if they can distinguish flavors. Ask students also to describe the tastes, using specific adjectives.

Bring in a homemade ice-cream machine and show the class the ingredients which go into ice cream. Give each student a sample of homemade and then store-bought ice cream and have them contrast the two for flavor, consistency and physical properties.

Make a tape recording of the class as they are noisily enjoying some ice cream. Afterwards, ask each student to write a possible script for an ice-cream party.

Read the poem "Eighteen Flavors," by Shel Silverstein in *Where the Sidewalk Ends*. Then ask the class to build, on paper, their own ice-cream cone with eighteen of their favorite flavors.

Build a huge class ice-cream cone! Each student chooses his favorite flavor, draws it on a large scoop of white paper and adds it to the two-foot cone on the bottom of the bulletin board. By the time the entire class has added their scoops, the ice-cream cone will probably be to the ceiling!

With your class complete the section on ice cream in the book *Secrets & Surprises* by Joe Wayman and Lorraine Plum (Carthage, IL: Good Apple, Inc., 1977).

Brainstorm, as a class, the answer to this question: What would you say to an ice-cream sundae? (Example of response: Are you busy on Saturday, too?)

Design a class bumper sticker in honor of Ice-Cream Day.

GA1154

I Scream for Ice-Cream Day!

Lucky Learner:

Invent a new flavor of ice cream by combining several different flavors already on the market.

Write an advice column response to the following letter:

Dear Mr./Miss Know-It-All,

I have this terrible problem. As soon as I get a triple decker ice-cream cone, instead of licking the ice cream from the top like you're supposed to do, I bite the bottom of the cone and suck all the ice cream out through the hole. The real problem comes when I suck so hard, the cone collapses and I get ice cream all over my face and clothes. What should I do?

Signed,
Conehead

If someone could make the perfect sundae, what different ingredients would it have to include? Draw the ideal sundae in life-size form.

List all the different kinds of food which contain ice cream.

Use this as a basis for a creative story:

Tubs of ice cream floated down the river as the storm threatened the area. As the chocolate marshmallow nut ice cream oozed out of its tub, some strawberry caramel and raisin dream cream met it and they . . . . Now finish the story!

Ice cream is as cold as . . . . Make a list!

Compose an advertising jingle for this new product: Butter Pecan Banana Chocolate Chip Surprise.

Invent a comic strip which features Iggy the Ice-Cream Cone and Felix the Fabulous Ice-Cream Float.

Write a tall tale which includes Choco the Ten-Foot Chocolate Popsicle and Smoothie the Forty-Five Flavor Sundae.

GA11

I Scream for Ice-Cream Day!

Lucky Learner:

Create an ice-cream delight using many different colors of clay, and write an eight-line humorous poem about it.

Brainstorm ten perfect times for eating ice cream.

Write a mystery story where the only clues are a half-eaten ice-cream cone, an empty ice-cream dish and an ice-cream bar wrapper.

Invent a new holiday which highlights ice cream.

Design a T-shirt which has the most delectable ice-cream concoction on the front.

Use one of these titles to inspire you to write a fascinating story, or make up a creative title of your own.

Ice-Cream Cones Invade the Mall
Ice Cream or Frozen Yogurt—Which Is Truly the Best?
He Screamed for His Ice Cream
Chocolate Shakes Ooze over the City
Ice Cream Ranks as Number One Favorite in the Nation
A New Flavor of Ice Cream Is Discovered

Take ordinary ice-cream delights like the chocolate sundae, strawberry float or the vanilla shake and create brand-new tantalizing names for these delectable taste creations which will really entice others to want to try them.

Instead of cones or dishes, think of some other possible containers for ice cream. (Example: a hot fudge sundae inside of a shoe)

GA1154

Ice-Cream Monster Attacks
Hot Fudge Fiend!

One teeth-chattering, frosty day in January, 1999, the Ice-Cream Monster was seen attacking household freezers, collecting enough ice cream to make sure he didn't melt away into the Never, Never Land of Vanishing Ice Cream and Evaporating Ice Milk, but rather live out his days in the Forever, Forever Land of Ice-Cream Heaven.

On this very same day, the Hot Fudge Fiend was making his rounds through the Neighborhood of Frozen Delights, in search of something onto which he could drizzle delicious chocolate droppings!

Well, as it just so happened, the Ice-Cream Monster was leaving Barry Butterfat's freezer when he ran smack dab into guess who? The Hot Fudge Fiend! The fiasco that followed was unbelievable!

Now it's time to finish this story! Be as creative and imaginative as you possibly can! Have fun!

_____

_____

_____

_____

_____

_____

_____

_____

GA115

Isabel Screams for Ice Cream!

Isabel Ireland ignored her doctor and ate gallons and gallons of ice cream every day. In addition, Isabel delivered ice cream and ice milk to the various businesses around town to keep her yummy habit paid for!

During one week, Isabel involved many different shops with her ice-cream delights. In Inner Inkwell, Iowa, Isabel inspired IBM with 142 gallons of peanut butter pecan ice cream and ITEK Corporation with 57 gallons of chocolate ice milk. Illusions purchased 29 gallons of strawberry and Independent Glass Company bought 62 gallons of fudge ripple. Images, Inc., decided on 11 gallons of caramel and 33 gallons of butterscotch. Innovative Designs took 71 gallons of butternut, while Ideal Plumbing wanted 54 gallons of chocolate marshmallow. Integrated Data Corporation bought 16 gallons of vanilla nut surprise and Inland Electronics ordered 28 gallons of vanilla-chocolate swirl. Interior Plant Designs purchased 4 gallons of raspberry dream ice cream, and Isabel sold 25 gallons of butter pecan to Interstate Transmissions.

Now the questions are exactly how many total gallons of ice cream and ice milk did Isabel sell and how many different flavors did the businesses buy?

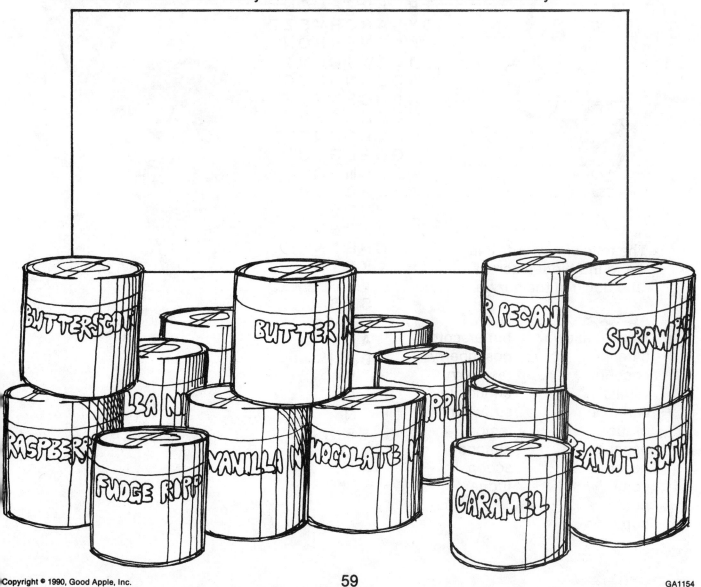

GA1154

Ice-Cream Delight

```
      L N J V J V N Z V M D
     K I K O J Z V W N D S B Z D P
    C A R A M E L V Z C O C O N U T L
   J O R A N G E S H C G J T L C F T F O
  A N Z C H V A N I L L A J F G C G N M
 Z X C F W C P E C A N W O W F C X K D B L
 Z S R U N O Q S C O N E V Q S E C U P G E
 T H V M A R S H M A L L O W S C D Q M E M
 F T I Y L B S S J H T F R I Y G M R S M O
 V F J R M N T C D B L U E B E R R Y B J N
 V B K O O J R O D R R F N U T S Z E N J P
 G V G V N O A O C A U F G F H B D E T V S
  T Z B D Z W P H S W B A N A N A C L N
   I Z F T B N O P W U S A S N Z N Z
    H F E S C B O T H K C U T
    O R J O E I T J H K I
    T R K L R Z E M C N H
    D Y S A R C R V S Z D
     K V T Y F S S O N
     J L E W J C D N T
     S D Z C N O P Z C
     N F H C B T F Y P
      U E H O C S R
      D V P S H N T
      G G R E G C O
      E X B N J C F
      T U R B F D B
       H N E S L
       J X R N X
      C H R F N
      I K Y T D
       V B P
       S J S
      O J M
      A U F
      B F H
       V
       B
       N
       F
```

The following words can be found hidden across and down in the puzzle.

ACROSS	DOWN
marshmallows	butterscotch
blueberry	bosenberry
coconut	raspberry
vanilla	chocolate
caramel	strawberry
orange	lemon
banana	almond
pecan	scoop
cone	fudge
nuts	
cup	

GA1154

It's a Clean Machine Monday!

Logical Leader:

Invite some individuals who have expertise with the different kinds of machines to share their knowledge with the students. Compare and contrast the information obtained from the guest speakers to determine all the similarities and differences between the various types of machines. Ask the class to prepare interview questions prior to their visits.

Create human machines by dividing the class up into small groups and assigning various machines to imitate. (Examples: sewing machine, typewriter, blender, etc.) Tell students that collectively their bodies are to become that machine. Then have them act out the "human machines" for the class and ask the others to try to guess what machines the groups are portraying.

Initiate some of the simple machine activities with your class which are on pages 75-77 in *The Good Apple Guide to Creative Drama* by Kathy U. Foley, Mara Lud and Carol Power (Carthage, IL: Good Apple, Inc., 1981).

Ask each person in the class to design his/her own simple machine, something which will actually make an unpleasant job much easier to do. Draw the machines on 5" × 8" index cards, both front and back. Then hang the cards on a class mobile.

Using cardboard, scissors and tape, ask students to design models of their favorite machines. Hold an artistic exhibit, where every class member walks around the room and evaluates each cardboard model in these areas: 1. resemblance to the machine itself, 2. amount of time and effort, 3. pride in workmanship. Be sure students are made aware of the evaluation criteria before they begin.

Rube Goldberg was a cartoonist who made very complex cartoons which depicted a series of actions and reactions, all aimed at showing a collection of contraptions which lead to one end or finale. Ask students to draw their own "Rube Goldbergs," keeping in mind the theme of the day—Machines. (For a further handout on Rube Goldberg and a picture example of his work, you might try the book *Inventions, Robots, Future* by The Learning Works, Inc., 1984, page 19.)

Ask the class what they might wittingly say to any machine you offer. (Example: What would you say to a telephone? Answer: Heard any good calls lately?)

Have your students write brain teasing riddles that revolve around machines. (Example: I'm a machine that changes temperature when I get plugged in. I'm used to taking the wrinkles out of clothing, and I work very well with water. What am I? Answer: an iron)

It's a Clean Machine Monday!

Lucky Learner:

Brainstorm all the different categories of machines there are in the world today. Make a list.

Think about the definition for the word *machine*. Next, look up the definition in the dictionary. Now try to think of a hierarchy from the very simplest of machines on up to the highest form of machines, the computer. Draw the hierarchy on a big piece of poster or tagboard.

Consider the names of five very different machines. (Example: computer, television, radio, stove and automobile) Write each name backwards and now you have the names of five new machines. Your job is to write a catalog description for each.

You decide to work late one night in the computer lab, but unfortunately, you are the only one there. As you start to program in your data, the lights on the central computer, KNOWITALL, start flashing off and on and cards start to fly everywhere! You don't know quite what to do so you . . . . Now finish the story!

Name all the things which could possibly go wrong with a radio, a TV or a stereo.

Make a list of all the different means by which machines can be powered. (Example: solar, electric, etc.)

Many machines make muncho megajobs much more manageable and meaningful for millions of mighty men every Monday morning. Now write your own machine-oriented tongue twister.

GA1154

It's a Clean Machine Monday!

Lucky Learner:

Which would you rather be—a simple machine like a can opener or a complex machine like a color computer? Why? Write your reasons in a short essay.

What would have changed in the world if machines had never been invented? Describe a day in your life without machines.

Imagine that you were inside a machine, looking out. Choose a specific machine and describe what you see.

You have just learned that in ten days all the machines in the world will be destroyed except three. Make a list of all the machines you use each week, and then prioritize them until you come up with the three you'll plan to save from destruction.

Many different and worthwhile jobs have been generated for people by machines. List all of the jobs which people hold solely for the purpose of working with a machine. Then make a list of all the jobs where people have been replaced by machines. Compare and contrast the two lists.

You have been given the special power to create the ultimate Magnificent Machine. What will this machine look like, do and how much will it cost to manufacture? Draw a detailed diagram.

Pretend that you could be any machine in the world. Which machine would you choose to be and why?

You are an undercover police person and are on assignment to discover who's been stealing the money out of the Coke and Pepsi machines at the local YMCA. Plan out your methods of attack on paper to discover who "dun" it.

Use one of the following titles to inspire you to write a creative story, or create one of your own:

Machines Run the World
The Day I Took a Machine to Lunch
More Machines Must Go!
A Machine Without Knobs
Snow Stereo and the Seven Speakers

GA1154

Mission: Possible

Machines are truly fascinating devices, and believe it or not, every single one of them has a story to tell! Details like when the machine was first invented, who the inventor was and the thinking that went into the machine's design all play an important part in the history of every machine we see around us today.

Now your mission, if you decide to take it, is to choose one of the machines listed below*, research it at the library and through your research, answer the following questions. Then choose a project to help you share your ideas with the class.

1. What was the date when the machine was invented?
2. Who invented the machine?
3. Is there a special story behind how or why it was invented?
4. What kind of market is there for the machine? In other words, who might use this machine?

If you are having difficulty answering some of these questions for a machine, simply choose a different one. After you have done all your research, choose from one of the projects below to incorporate the ideas you found.

biographical poem	display	model
ballad	fact file	mini center
adventure story	essay	mobile
brochure	videotape	photo essay
demonstration	flow chart	crossword puzzle

Samples of machines to choose from

computer	sewing machine	electric saw	camera
hair dryer	stereo	VCR	telephone
microwave	stove	spa	cotton gin
blender	TV	motorboat	airplane
electric can opener	typewriter	automobile	

*Feel free to research any other machine which might be of interest to you.

Marvelous Monster Monday

Logical Leader:

Read "Monsters I've Met" in Shel Silverstein's *A Light in the Attic*. Have the students write about imaginary monsters they've met in their lives and what kind of an impact they have had on them. If they've never met one, have them make one up, on the spot.

With your class, complete the creative dramatics activities on monsters in the book *Secrets & Surprises* by Joe Wayman and Lorraine Plum (Carthage, IL: Good Apple, Inc., 1977).

Give everyone in your class pieces of felt on which they are to create flannel board monsters. The monsters can be really jazzed up with sequins and paints and other pieces of felt. Put all the monsters together and create a flannel board story entitled "The Day the Monsters Came to Town."

Read the following to your students:

> The Loch Ness Monster and Big Foot are just two of the very famous monsters which have supposedly been seen by many individuals at various times. Imagine that a semi-friendly monster moved into the trailer court on your block and came out only at night to make friends. The problem was and still is that the only way it knows to meet people is by blowing its lips into a giant French horn and watching the reactions of others. What do the neighbors say? Write a story which will solve everyone's problem.

Cut a very long piece of light-colored butcher paper. Allowing one foot by three feet for each child, ask each student to draw a "full-length" monster, which will stand side by side with his classmates', until the mural is complete with a series of tall and unique monsters done by all members of the class. Entitle it "I Never Met a Monster I Didn't Like!" and hang it on your wall.

Collectively write a monstrous adventure which might begin with this line:

In a very dark alley, a huge black shape moved silently among the shadows.

Now, ask one student to give the class the next line in the adventure, and then the next child adds his line and so on until everyone has added a really "creative" line to the adventure. Brainstorm titles until the class comes up with one they really like and voila! One monstrous adventure coming up!

Design monster flip books with the kids! Everyone staples six to ten index cards or quarter sheets of blank page on one side like little mini books. Now ask the students to draw six consecutive pictures, one per page, which show a monster engaged in some type of feat. Then the books can be "flipped" to tell a monstrous story!

GA1154

Marvelous Monster Monday

Lucky Learner:

Brainstorm all the monsters you've ever heard about, read about, seen on TV shows or movies or discovered elsewhere. Then choose ten of your favorites and pick one characteristic from each. Design a "super" monster, using all of those characteristics, give it a name and write a short story about its haunts.

In what ways can you relieve a small child's fears about monsters?

Create imaginary recipes for Monster Mash, Monster Soup and Monster Mousse.

What would happen if a monster were elected President? How would the United States government be different? Make a list of all the ways.

Create a monster machine which will design a different kind of monster each time it is fed a one million dollar bill.

Food is to humans as WHAT is to monsters?

What different events would be similar to a small army of monsters invading a drive-in movie? Make a list of at least five events.

Frankenstein was a man-made monster, and Dr. Jekyll became Mr. Hyde after he drank a secret potion. List all of the ways you can think of for a monster to become a monster.

If you were a monster and could be of one benefit to society, which benefit would it be and why?

Using only geometric shapes (circles, squares, rectangles, triangles, etc.), create a multi-colored monster with mounds of hair! Use markers to add details.

GA1154

Marvelous Monster Monday

Lucky Learner:

We all know how traditional monsters are supposed to look. But your job is to create a monster so unlike any which has ever been thought of before, that you will be proclaimed "Master Monster Maker of the Universe!"

How might a monster react to a mirror? Or to a barking beagle? Or to a hot air balloon? Or to a flashlight in its face? Or to a ghost? Make a list of your responses.

If you turned a monster inside out, what would you get? Draw it!

"Many monsters march a military mile in the middle of midwestern Minnesota." Now write your own tongue twister around the letter *M*.

List five ways to measure the height and weight of an unseen monster.

What *ing* word would best describe what monsters do when they feel worried? Happy? Scared? Hopeful? Depressed? Write about these feelings and their ultimate actions.

Write an adventure story about Melvin the Mustard Monster and his fight to keep the Ketchup King out of town.

Create a telegram which would be sent from a little boy to his pet monster, who has run away from home.

If a monster could sing, what would he sound like? What would his favorite song be? Compose the "perfect" monster song.

Create a monster maze, where math problems have to be solved to get to the center or finish line.

67

Monster Match!

To create one of the greatest monster stories ever written, put together one choice from each column below and let your imagination run wild! Mix and match and the wilder the better!

Who?	What?	Where?	When?	Why?
Cyclops	flood	at a sports meet	21st C.	thrills
Loch Ness	parade	on a bicycle	1492 AD	money
Big Foot	letter	over a mountain	last year	power
Sea Serpent	baseball game	under a waterfall	tomorrow	happiness
Abominable Snowman	plane ride	in the Antarctic	in 10 years	anger
Headless Horseman	wedding	at the movies	during the past 5 minutes	as a joke
King Kong	rodeo	on a train	100 AD	glory
Frankenstein	Disneyland	at a video arcade	next week	challenge

(Example: Big Foot, at a baseball game, was seen riding a bicycle during the last five minutes, and he looked like it was a big fat joke . . . .)

GA1154

Monster Madness

One magnificent Monday in May, a munchkin monster named Monroe molted and became Mighty Mo, the meanest, moldiest and most monotonous monster monarch in the history of mankind! Mighty Mo moved many a monument in his day while humming a melancholy melody along his way. As one May moon rose, a morsel of monument lay in Mighty Mo's path, so Mo munched it down in a minute.

On his way to the mall, Mighty Mo met and munched down 327 more morsels of monument before Mo's mouth became muffled and immovable. Much as Mighty Mo tried to mutter and mumble, his mouth muscles were mute. Many other monsters tried to medicate Mighty Mo and some even tried to feed Mighty Mo melba toast and mini melon balls but with no luck. This meant that Mighty Mo's mouth was to forever remain shut.

Now, if each morsel of monument that Mighty Mo munched weighed four ounces, how many pounds did all those morsels together weigh? (Multiplication, division, measurement)

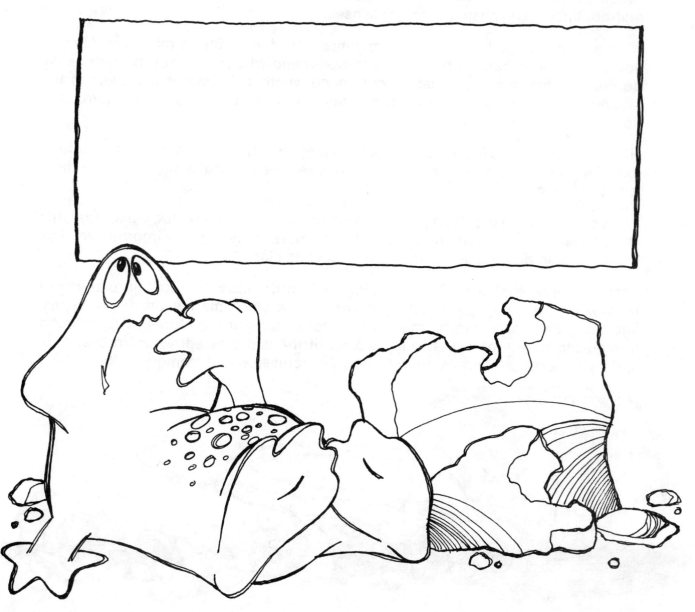

GA1154

Naturally Nutty Wednesday

Logical Leader:

Have the class, in small groups, write and perform "peanut" plays, where all the characters portray nuts.

Complete a taste test between crunchy and smooth peanut butter. One way to accomplish this might be to give students quarters of smooth peanut butter sandwichs and quarters of crunchy peanut butter sandwichs and ask them to write descriptive paragraphs about the quality of each sandwich's taste.

Read "Peanut Butter Sandwich" in Shel Silverstein's *Where the Sidewalk Ends*. Ask students to write six-line stanzas about the best time they ever had while eating peanut butter sandwiches.

Share the encyclopedia entries for some of the less common nuts (macadamia, Brazil, pecans, pistachios, etc.) with the class. Ask students to conduct a compare-and-contrast survey, using their five senses.

"Sometimes you feel like a nut, sometimes you don't." Share miniature Almond Joy and Mounds bars with students to determine whether or not the nuts really do make a difference and also to determine whether the statement made in the Mounds and Almond Joy's advertisements is true for students on this particular day.

Have the class create Nut Art by decorating large nutshells with markers and writing four-line humorous poems about what they've created. Make sure to share them with the class.

Write class or small group jingles which advertise a new kind of nut, which students should name and which should be both humorous as well as informative. The jingles should be sung and performed before the class.

Create a game similar to Concentration, only with cards that contain pictures of nuts. A simple gameboard can be drawn with a black marker on empty boxes, and the game cards can be made from index cards and pictures of nuts found in magazines. The object is to lay out all of the cards facedown, turn over two, and try for a match. This game will certainly increase visual memory skills.

GA1154

Naturally Nutty Wednesday

Lucky Learner:

We've all looked at a nut from the outside in. Think about what the inside of a nutshell must look like. Draw a picture.

Take the names of six nuts: pecan, walnut, pistachio, peanut, Brazil nut and almond. Using only the letters in those words, make up the names of foods which contain nuts. Only use the letters as many times collectively as they appear in the words.

One pistachio day in Peanut Land, a small walnut named Willie went to see his best friend, Arnold Almond. Willie and Arnold were concerned because the Pecan Brothers, Peter and Paul, were building a house out of peanut brittle, peanut butter and pecans, but were leaving the almonds and walnuts completely out of it. When they got there, Willie and Arnold found . . . . **Now creatively finish the story!**

You are a scientist and have been given the job of developing a "bionic nut," using any and all resources available. Develop the nut on paper and present it to the class.

A poor little nut has lost its shell and can't find its way back home. Think of three things to tell the baby nut to help him find his way.

Basically, nuts themselves are very plain. **Name at least ten things you could do to spruce them up.**

How do nuts learn to be so crazy? They must have gone to a pretty nutty school! Write a few paragraphs about the Super Silly School for Nuts.

Invent a peanut pleaser, a contraption which, when turned on, will please people by using peanuts in some very unusual way.

GA1154

Naturally Nutty Wednesday

Lucky Learner:

Invent ten new uses for nuts.

Write a conversation which might occur between a peanut and a stick of butter.

Brainstorm all the different meanings for the word *nut.*

Compose a nut narrative (story) using one of the following titles or making up one of your own creative titles:

       Three Nuts in a Shell
       Peanuts Take Pride in Packaging
       Nuts Across America
       Peanut Butter Builds Better Bodies
       Peanuts Please Principals
       Walnuts Waste Watermelons
       Pecans Plan Party

What would happen if a peanut and a walnut were ever mixed? Draw the results. What new taste would you have and what would you call it?

Write a funny joke about the "nut that was one of a kind."

Compose an "Ode to Nuts."

Combine a photograph, a tape recorder, a peanut and a doll into an original invention. Draw it.

Invent your own "nutty" food. Imagine the recipe for this new concoction and write it down.

Give a demonstration, showing at least five ways to get peanut butter off the roof of your mouth.

GA1154

Leopardo Ma Binci,
Greatest Inventor Alive!

You are now Leopardo Ma Binci, the greatest inventor to have ever lived. One of your greatest inventions was the landoplane, a vehicle that made travel on land much quicker and much more comfortable.

At this time, you are being given a new challenge: how to combine a photograph, a tape recorder, a peanut and a doll into an unusual and unique invention unlike any the world has ever seen. Leopardo, good luck in this exciting venture, and draw a blueprint of this new contraption below!

a photograph + a tape recorder + a peanut + a doll = ?

GA1154

Naturally Nutty

As normally nutty nights go, this night was unbelievably nutty! You see, Peter Peanut and Wilfred Walnut were on their way to the Pick a Nut Dance, where they met Albert Almond, Paul Pistachio, Mort Macadamia, Preston Pecan and Bobby Brazil Nut. All the stud nuts loved to dance and asked each of the twenty-seven girl nuts who attended to dance with them at least once.

Some of the dances included the Walnut Waltz, Peanut Polka, Brazil Nut Boogie, Macadamia Muscle Man Strut and the Pecan Pogo.

After each nut danced with a fair maiden nut, he took her over to the refreshment table. Some of the nutty delicacies included Brazil Nut Pudding, Almond Joy Surprise, Peanut Butter Brownies, Butter Pecan Ice Cream, Green Pistachio Delight and Macadamia Nut Souffle.

Now the nutty question is, if each male nut danced with each of the attending female nuts one time apiece, how many total dances would that be? (Simple multiplication, whole numbers)

GA1154

No Nutty Nonsense!

Using your greatest imagination, creativity and humor, answer the following nonsense questions, keeping in mind the theme of Nuts. Make sure your answers are as complete as possible. Have fun!

1. What would you say to a pistachiobeano?

2. How would you dance with a Brazilnutanterian?

3. What kind of dinner would you cook for a walnutito?

4. Describe a pecanoctagonnie's home.

5. What is a peanutgrummy's favorite video game? Why?

6. Which books are Almondrunt's favorites?

7. Macadamiapps love which circus acts?

8. Cashewrhinoflaps hang around with what other nuts?

9. What else does a pistachiombleep do besides bleep?

10. Where in the world does a Brazilnutaholic live and work?

11. Which rides at the amusement park do pecanolios like?

12. Who are Sweptalmond's best friends?

13. Which plants do rashoocashews eat?

14. What kind of work does a peanutdoodle do?

15. Where would a Brazilnuttoo wear her jewelry?

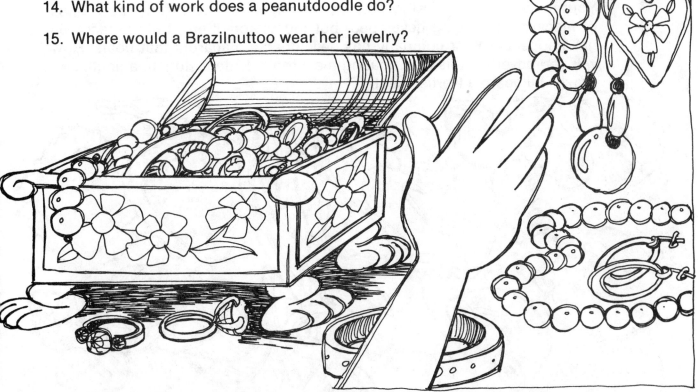

75

GA1154

No Bologna, It's Macaroni Day!

Logical Leader:

Present the class with at least five different types of pasta, and ask them to compare and contrast the pasta on a chart, using all five of their senses.

Invite a mother or grandmother who makes homemade pasta into the classroom to explain the process to the class.

Bring in some cooked spaghetti noodles and give each student a small portion. The object is to have everyone invent a new way to eat spaghetti.

One hundred yards of spaghetti were eaten in 12.02 seconds on July 3, 1986, by Peter Dowdeswell. Hold a spaghetti-eating contest to see who can eat the most spaghetti in a given amount of time.

Read the poem entitled "Spaghetti" in Shel Silverstein's book *Where the Sidewalk Ends*, inspiring visions of your students' own experiences with spaghetti. Ask the class to write about real or imaginary spaghetti experiences in poetic verse.

Place different types of noodles in cups, one noodle per cup. Cover the cups and ask classmates which kind of noodle is which, using their keen powers of observation and strictly by shaking the cup and listening to the sounds the noodles make.

Create macaroni art by using various-shaped hard noodles and gluing them into artistic designs. Use markers and crayons to add additional details, and poster paint to color the macaroni in wild and fancy shades.

Ask the class to list at least eight other food items which, when mixed with pasta might make a very fine meal. (Example: meatballs, cheddar cheese, etc.)

Pose this statement to your class:

> You are the Macaroni King (Queen) of the world. Every day, new kinds of macaroni are being developed, but today, something truly miraculous has happened! Your company has developed a macaroni that floats! How will you advertise this new floating macaroni? Write a slogan, a jingle and draw a billboard advertisement.

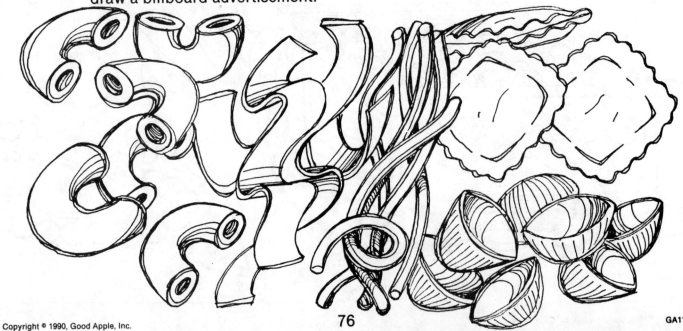

GA1154

No Bologna, It's Macaroni Day!

Lucky Learner:

Compose paragraphs describing how macaroni and cheese could be improved.

Write *MACARONI* vertically and use each letter to begin a word or phrase which describes macaroni. (In other words, a name poem)

There is a new kind of animal just recently discovered called a macaroonie, which lives in the mountains of Italy and eats spoonies of macaroons in its sleep. Write a make-believe story about the macaroonies and how they got to America.

Write a conversation which might occur between a piece of spaghetti and a curly pasta noodle.

Create a short TV script where the main characters are Melvin the Macaroni King of Pasta and Esmerelda the Macaroni Fairy.

Write and present a mini play about an Italian grandmother, her love for pasta, and how that love gets her into trouble.

Use different pieces of raw pasta noodles to create art objects, noodle pictures or even jewelry.

Besides just for eating, list all the other things for which macaroni could be used.

What if your best friend were a piece of macaroni? Write a funny story about your relationship.

How could you improve a pasta noodle? Name five different ways.

 GA1154

No Bologna, It's Macaroni Day!

Lucky Learner:

Imagine that macaroni could stand up and walk on its own accord. Where do you think it would go and what do you think it would do when it got there?

All of a sudden, the world was overflowing with macaroni noodles and spaghetti and ravioli and everyone was running for cover. What would you do if you were caught in this situation?

Invent three new recipes which contain noodles, or find three recipes in a cookbook which contain noodles in someone's cookbook.

Make up a story about how macaroni noodles lost their curl.

An abbreviation for macaroni is Mac, which is also the nickname for a person. Make a list of all the other foods which contain a syllable that is also a person's name or nickname.

Spaghetti-O's, Macaroni-O's and Noodle-O's are all on or have been on the food market recently. If you could make a canned or boxed foodstuff with noodles, what would you call it? Think of at least ten different names.

If you were on a deserted island and the only thing that washed ashore was a trunk filled with boxes of macaroni and cheese, how would you prepare it? Write specific directions.

You are a scientist and have just been told that there is a secret plot to replace all natural macaroni with artificial noodles and that even as we speak, the enemy is infiltrating the country. What kinds of tests would you devise to test the noodles to determine if they were real or fake?

What would happen if macaroni grew on trees and every time a tree was watered, it grew an inch? What would a macaroni orchard look like? Draw a picture of your perception.

List all of the ways life would be different if we didn't have macaroni.

GA1154

What If?

The following "What If?" questions are aimed at peaking your curiosity and poking at your creativity. Answer each one using as much imagination as you can muster! No answer is too wild or off the wall! Have fun and think unique!

What if a giant piece of macaroni . . .

1. Believed that he was the real tooth fairy?

2. Loved to smile and wanted to be photographed with you and your family?

3. Was given to you as your new pet?

4. Joined your baseball team?

5. Was caught in your bathtub?

6. Wanted to baby-sit your younger brother or sister?

7. Could fix your bicycle?

8. Was a member of a rock and roll band?

9. Had a cage at the zoo?

10. Stopped a burglar from entering your home?

11. Had great seats for the circus?

12. Was a miniature amusement park ride?

13. Could do all your homework?

14. Pretended he was your best friend?

15. Was a king in disguise?

GA1154

Monkeys Munch Macaroni

Millions of monkeys eat macaroni every minute of the new moon, right after midnight, while making melon balls and mushroom meat loaf for their moms. It's no mistake that Melvin the Monkey missed his mark when he mustered up some minestrone instead and, moreover, made his mom miserable for many months.

Monkeys make marvelous macaroni by using a miraculous new recipe which monsters maintain is the most tasty ever made. The macaroni raises their metabolism and then Merlin the Magician messes around with their imaginations.

One Monday, a mess of monkeys totaling fifty made off with three plates of macaroni apiece before a monk from the monastery made a call to Merlin. Merlin performed three tricks an hour for nine hours before he munched his five plates of macaroni, as well.

There were only two problems to be solved. Just exactly how many plates of macaroni were totally eaten, and how many tricks did Merlin do for the monkeys that moonlit evening? (Addition, multiplication, whole numbers)

GA11

Perfectly Pickled Friday!

Logical Leader:

Hand out one pickle per student. Have students name their pickles, as well as write physical descriptions of them, using lots of adjectives and the five senses' descriptors. (Example: It feels like . . . . It sounds like . . . , etc.)

Design art projects with the pickles, using toothpicks, marshmallows, gumdrops, olives, Gummy Bear snakes, etc. Or pose this idea to your class: Percy Pickle fell down a hill and when he got up, nothing was quite the same. How does Percy look now?

Read "Ickle Me, Pickle Me, Tickle Me, Too" in Shel Silverstein's *Where the Sidewalk Ends*. Ask students to write poems which in some way include the word *pickle* or the idea of pickles.

Use a pickle recipe to turn small dill cucumbers into pickles. Make it a class project by dividing students into groups and assigning different duties to each group. Store the pickles for about two months and then share them with the class.

As a class, compose the "Ballad of the Pickle."

Construct a class mobile which depicts all the different kinds of pickles there are on the market today.

Share the encyclopedia entry for pickles, the process by which they are made and the different varieties available with the class. Discuss the information given and quiz class members to see what they've retained.

Create a giant class jigsaw puzzle of a super-sized pickle, using a large piece of cardboard and green markers and crayons. Ask one student who is artistically inclined to draw the Super Pickle, both on the cardboard and on a piece of blank paper, and then class members can take turns coloring in the cardboard pickle. Laminate and cut the Super Pickle into puzzle pieces. Classmates can take turns putting the Super Pickle Puzzle together!

Design a series of pickle greeting cards with the class. Every student is given a blank card and is told to write a poem using the "pickle and greeting card" theme. Cards are to be designed in the pickle motif and the greeting is to go on the inside.

GA1154

Perfectly Pickled Friday!

Lucky Learner:

Create pickle prose, using either one of the following titles or by creating one of your own:

       The Pickle Monster Meets His Maker
       A Pickle and a Peck Around the Wreck
       Pickles Pride in Tickling Pretty Peas
       Pirate Pickles to the Rescue

For what else could a pickle be used besides food? Make a list.

Combine a pickle, a hammer, a paper clip and a computer keyboard. What do you get? Draw it! Then write an advertising jingle for it.

Create a comic strip about Paully Pickle and his pet panda, Penelope.

Write a slogan to help sell the very new "Super Pickle!"

Complete a survey of people and their preferences for pickles. Compile the results.

Write a newspaper article about "The Pickle That Saved the World!"

Create a crossword puzzle about and in the shape of a pickle.

Compose a humorous rhyme about the sweet pickle turned dill.

Design a name poem for one of the many different types of pickles.

GA11

Perfectly Pickled Friday!

Lucky Learner:

Using only the letters in the word *pickle* and using each letter as many times as you'd like, create a colorful artistic design.

A spring day brought out all kinds of unusual creatures, one of which was the little renowned Pickle Person. Her name was Paula, and she was so incredibly different that everyone made fun of her. She felt very bad, for you see, all Paula Pickle ever wanted to do was to make friends.

So every morning, Paula went on a long journey to try to see what friends she could make. But by the end of the day, she always came home empty-handed.

Then one summer's day, Paula set out on her daily walk, when suddenly, something truly incredible happened!

Now you finish the story!

How do pickles learn to be sour? How do they stay sweet? Write a diary entry about a sweet and a dill pickles' first day at the Preppy Pickle School.

What would happen if you were a pickle? Would you be sweet or dill? How does it feel to be surrrounded by others exactly like you? What do you do in your jar to occupy your time until you're chosen to be eaten? And how do you feel about being eaten? Write a one-page essay expressing your thoughts on these questions.

Pickles must be born in jars, just as tapes are born inside a VCR. Name at least ten inanimate objects that tell how they came to be. (Example: Record albums are born in their covers.)

Think of something sour. Now think of something sweet. Combine the two and you have just discovered a pickly new taste sensation. Name it, package it (on paper) and try to sell it to the class.

Draw a pickleorange, a pickleoozie or a fuzziepickle.

Write at least ten adjectives which describe pickles.

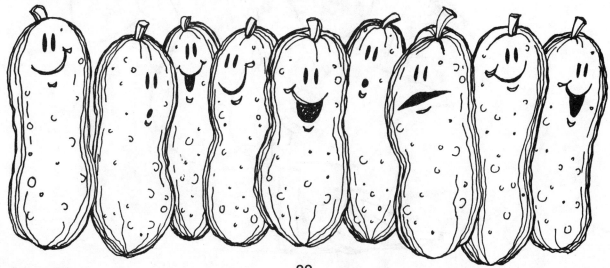

Some Pickley Stories

Below are presented several story starters which will allow you to choose one and write a very creative and imaginative story about pickles. Feel free to mix and match the ideas before you make your final story-idea decision. Have fun!

Paulette Pickle and her friend, Pistol Pete, were engaged in an intriguing mystery, but no one was to find out about . . . .

The private pickle, Captain Pepe, overtook the entire ship before the totally unexpected happened . . . .

A large green pickle, Mrs. Vertigo, ran her classroom with an iron finger, until she made that one big mistake . . . .

The basketball team, the Harlem Pickletrotters, had completed another successful game when suddenly . . . .

The picklemobile was off in space, with pickle-astronauts Paul and Paulette at the wheel, when a small red button started to blink . . . .

The main town pickle theatre was full. It was Friday night and the movie was running, when suddenly the fire alarm went off and . . . .

Sadly, Patty Pickle broke up with Preston Pickle and was very upset and disappointed until . . . .

In the country, the pickle dill was ready for action, a six-pickle on his belt . . . .

Prince and Princess Pickle ruled the kingdom with a forceful hand, that was until the day that he came into town . . . .

The pickle clown performed many tricks before the terribly unexpected accident occurred . . . .

84

A Pickle for Your Thoughts!

Honestly answer each of the following questions. Make your answers as complete as possible and always tell why you answered the way you did. Although the questions may seem humorous at first, they also can point out some very interesting ideas, if you really ponder them for a minute or two. Have fun, and a pickle for your thoughts!

Which is brighter—
a pickle on fire or an A+ student?

Which is faster—
a pickaholic with a jar of pickles or "time" when you're in trouble?

Which is colder—
a frozen pickle on a stick or a stare?

Which is longer—
super pickle or a tape measure?

Which hurts more—
a chatty pickle who talks behind your back or a bad sunburn?

Which is more bizarre—
a pickle in a clown suit or Batman getting arrested for batting?

Which is funnier—
pickles in Nike shoes or a practical joke?

Which is smoother—
a baby gherkin's skin or a clean floor?

Which is more talented—
a pickle who can juggle three bowling pins off its nose or an Olympic gold medalist?

Which is sadder—
a whimpering, crying pickle baby or the loss of something valued?

Which is sweeter—
a sweet pickle or a very nice elderly grandparent?

Which is more painful—
a pickle who tells a lie or an untrue friend?

Which is more lasting—
a big beautiful dill pickle or guilt?

GA1154

Pig Out! It's Pizza Day!

Logical Leader:

The largest pizza ever baked measured 86' 7" in diameter and 5895 square feet in area. Create a class-size pizza where everyone receives his or her very own area to decorate. Have an assortment of toppings on hand and ask students to be thinking of a name for this great creation. Then dig in!

Invite into your classroom an Italian family who either owns or has an interest in their own pizzeria to explain to the class how pizza is actually made. After they've left, ask students to draw flow charts, displaying the step-by-step process by which pizza is created.

Encourage the class to break up into small groups to write mini plays about "The Wonderful World of Pizza."

Write a class song entitled "When the Sun Hits Your Eye Like a Big Pizza Pie, It's Blinding."

Secure to your chalkboard or bulletin board a large piece of lightly colored butcher paper. Write "Pizza Graffiti" at the top, and try to elicit from the class all the words that in any way relate to pizzas and the fun times which surround them. Take the graffiti words and cut them apart into small stacks, one stack for each small group in the class. Students have the choice of turning the graffiti into either a radio script, a mini play, a poem, a sonnet or a short story. All finished products should be shared with the class.

Pose the logic problem on page 89 to your class and walk them through it. Once they see how easy it is, they'll have little difficulty completing logic problems in the future.

Ask students to write creative excuses they might give to their parents if they wanted to go to the local pizzeria but were grounded by their parents.

Create skywriting messages with your students which advertise student-invented pizza parlors and their upcoming grand openings!

An original type of pizza is being made in your town and it is your students' job to broadcast this delectable taste sensation to the public. Students can first write their broadcast script (remembering the who, what, when, where, why, how) and then take turns presenting their broadcasts in front of the class.

GA1

Pig Out! It's Pizza Day!

Lucky Learner:

List all of the toppings currently used on pizzas. Then brainstorm a list of other possible foods which might also make successful toppings. (Example: jelly beans or chocolate chips)

Invent a new kind of pizza. Draw it in full color and make it the actual size.

Design pizza guidebooks, stating the "proper" ways to eat different types of pizza. (Example: Pepperoni, double cheese pizza should only be eaten with a forked spoon as it needs to be slowly swirled and then gently brought in for the bite.)

Illustrate a cartoon which depicts life in a pizza parlor right after the team wins the big game.

Design a creative story, using one of these titles or make up one of your own:

   The Pepperoni Pizza Landed on Paul's Head
   Pizzas as Far as the Eyes Could See
   A Fairy-Tale Pizza Story Come True
   A Pickle, Pizza and Poem Solve the Case
   The Land of Pizza Princes and Princesses
   Pizzas Take over the World
   The Pizza That Was Too Hot to Handle

Compose an ode to your favorite pizza, and in it state why it is so special.

Develop a new flag which symbolizes Pizza Day.

The most pizza ever eaten in the shortest amount of time was 1.8 pounds in five minutes, twenty-three seconds. If you had an unlimited amount of your favorite pizza, imagine yourself in a short story, setting an all-new world's record!

Create a hidden picture, where at least fifteen pizzas are camouflaged by the overall picture. Share with classmates to see if they can discover the location of all of the pizzas.

Pig Out! It's Pizza Day!

Lucky Learner:

The case began at the local pizzeria where it was discovered that five boxes of pepperoni and sausage pizza were missing. The only clues left behind were a half-eaten piece of pizza, a key and a pizza box with the letter *M* scrawled across the top. You are Detective Quiggly, and you must solve the case before the pizza gets cold. Good luck!

Design a jigsaw puzzle of a giant pizza on cardboard. Laminate and cut into pieces large enough for a smaller child to handle.

Write a fantasy about a trip to the biggest pizzeria in the country and express just how all those delicious aromas cause you to do something truly remarkable. (Now just what was it?)

Conduct a survey in our neighborhood to determine the following: who eats pizza, what kinds of pizza are being eaten, how many times each week is pizza consumed by each family and in how many individual households is pizza the favorite food. Share the results of your survey with the class.

Create a story about little Pierre, who loved pizza so much he used to hoard it in his bedroom. Normally, Pierre ate every single pizza piece, but on this one Friday, he left one piece of mushroom, pepperoni, sausage, olive, anchovy, pimento, green pepper and double cheese pizza under his bed and completely forgot about it. A few months later, something quite extraordinary began to grow in Pierre's room, until finally it . . . . Now finish the story.

You own Pernelli's Pizzaria, and you wish to make a commerical to advertise your incredible meatball pizza. Write a pizza-winning slogan which will make the commercial complete.

Write a five-line limerick about a girl named Peggy and her suspicious past with pizzas.

Create a giant postage stamp to commemorate Pizza Day.

Design a secret word find in the shape of a pizza, using at least ten words which relate to pizza.

GA1▪

A Pizza Problem Eats Away!

Using the chart below, see if you can solve the logic problem presented here. Every time you figure out a girl, a pizza, an amount of time and/or a musical preference match, put a circle in the appropriate box. Then at the same time, place X's in all the squares vertically and horizontally from the O, which should make the rest of the solving much easier. Good luck!

Logical Problem:
There were three girls named Patty, Pixie and Penelope who loved three different types of pizza: cheese, pepperoni and sausage. One spent two hours, one spent four hours and one spent six hours in the pizzeria each day listening to PAL, Pasley Meadow or Pinkey Lee. Your job is to discover which girl loved which pizza and spent how many hours in the pizzeria listening to which musician.

Clues:
Pixie hates pepperoni and Patty hates cheese pizza.
Penelope has never heard PAL or Pinkey Lee.
Patty has to stay home most of the day.
Patty loves sausages.
Penelope spends most of her time at the pizzeria.
Pixie's favorite singer's initials are P.L.

	Cheese	Sausage	Pepperoni	2	4	6	PAL	Pasley Meadow	Pinkey Lee
Patty									
Pixie									
Penelope									

89

GA1154

Lucky Pizza Day!

In the next ten minutes, use your imagination and write the answers to the following problems, all relating to pizza. Have fun!

1. Add: 1 pizza plus 2 pizzas plus 3 pizzas plus 4 pizzas plus 5 pizzas plus 6 pizzas plus 7 pizzas plus 8 pizzas plus 9 pizzas plus 10 pizzas equals _____.

2. Write all the ingredients you can think of which are contained in one pizza.

3. Create three math story problems which all relate to pizzas. (Example: Sally had 12 pizzas and Wally ate 8. How many pizzas were left? Answer: 4)

4. If one pizza that you ordered grew to be as big as your house, what would you do?

5. List the names of five other foods which also begin with the letter P.

6. Draw the perfect pizza on a piece of blank white paper.

GA1154

Pop, Pop, Popcorn Day!

Logical Leader:

Pop up some popcorn for the class. Give everyone a full cup and ask each student to examine carefully one large kernel of corn. Allow students to draw the kernel in enlarged size, making note of every single detail. Crayons and colored pencils can help add details to the drawings.

Ask the class to try some different brands of popcorn which you've brought in and determine certain criteria which will help them select the best brand.

Present the creative dramatics activities on popcorn to the class on page 78 of the book *Secrets & Surprises* by Joe Wayman and Lorraine Plum (Carthage, IL, Good Apple, Inc., 1977).

Give students a little bit of caramel corn, cheese corn, candy corn and regular popcorn. Ask them to conduct a taste test comparison between the four, as well as a contrast in physical appearance, touch, smell and sound as they are being munched.

Invite a popcorn manufacturer into the classroom to explain to the class how they breed corn to produce the very best popcorn possible.

Encourage the class to write either name poems, cinquains or limericks about chocolate-covered popcorn.

Give the class the following ailments and ask them to invent a cure for each: popcornaphobia, kernelitis and cornmania.

Write riddles or jokes with your class about the origin of popcorn.

Using white or yellow socks, create popcorn puppets! Write "corny" scripts and present "poppet" (puppet) shows to the class.

Take the class on a fantasy trip to Popcorn Land, where all kinds of imaginary snack creatures will pop out at a moment's notice! Ask the class to brainstorm all the things that might be found on a fantasy trip of this kind and then synthesize them together and read the "trip" aloud.

GA1154

Pop, Pop, Popcorn Day!

Logical Leader:

You are sitting at home one night alone and decide to have some popcorn with your TV movie. You put the oil and the popcorn in the popper in the kitchen and then go back into the living room. You become so engrossed in the movie that you forget all about the popcorn. By the time you return to the kitchen, the popcorn popper is exploding and popcorn is everywhere! Your parents will be home in fifteen minutes! Write your way out of this mess!

Design a travel brochure to Popcorn City, Maine.

Caramel corn, cheese corn, candy corn and butter-flavored popcorn are all differently flavored versions of the same thing. Invent a new flavor of popcorn which will be relatively easy to make.

Write a speech, stating the pros and cons of popcorn consumption.

Create an advertisement for a brand-new kind of popcorn, complete with a slogan and a package.

Compose a series of chants or cheers which promote the different brands and kinds of popcorn.

Write a newspaper article which focuses in on the Popcorn Cowboy, a hero-like buccaneer who searched the world over for the perfect popcorn. (Don't forget to answer the who, what, where, when, why, how questions.)

Develop a logic problem which includes four different flavors of popcorn, four boys, four girls and four dentists.

Prepare a clay model of a popcorn kernel.

Describe popcorn using as many words as possible which end in *-ed* and *-ing*.

GA1154

Pop, Pop, Popcorn Day!

Lucky Learner:

Pretend that your favorite pet is a piece of popcorn. Create a "How to Care for Your Pet" Manual.

Popcorn spelled backwards is nrocpop, a strange and unusual new kind of snack eaten while walking in New Zealand. Compile a list of ten other unusual snacks made of corn.

If you could add something really special and unique to popcorn, what would it be and why?

What if popcorn could grow to be as tall as a building and as heavy as a two-ton truck? How would a night out at a drive-in theatre change?

Name five food dishes to which the ingredient popcorn would be a welcome addition.

Make up a story about the giant popcorn ball, rolling from town to town, looking for drive-in movies to haunt.

Add popcorn to a rock and what do you get? Combine popcorn with gum, a German shepherd dog, spaghetti and a feather and what do you get? Draw the new creation.

Write about when in your life popcorn did or really would have added to the festivities.

How many different ways can you make popcorn? Make a list!

Use one of these titles or one of your own to create an exciting popcorn tale:

    Popcorn Pops to the Sky
    A Piece of Popcorn Got Stuck in My Tooth
    The Popcorn Muncher's World Recrod
    Popcorn Sales Reach an All-Time Low
    Pick a Peck of Popcorn

GA1154

Pondering Popcorn

While pondering on a popcorn kernel, ask yourself these questions and see how many answers you can generate. Have fun!

How many ways can you think of to change the appearance of popcorn?

What would you do if a kernel of popcorn grew to be as big as your house and it decided it liked it there and wanted to stay?

What might happen if some popcorn fell onto the floor and then down fell some pop and pretty soon in walked your mom?

What would a popcorn kernel say to a salt container?

Which is crazier, someone trying to carry eight buckets of popcorn into the theatre at the same time or someone trying to stick a whole popcorn ball into his mouth at once? Why?

How would you cure a popcornaholic?

Write about the funniest time you ever spent with popcorn, real or imaginary.

How would you illustrate a popcorn ball that was especially beautiful?

Invent three ways to package popcorn.

If you were a popcornahologist, what kind of solution would you find for the rapidly rising costs of popcorn in theatres today?

Paula Peacock's Popcorn Products

Paula Peacock, a popcorn proprietor in Pittsburgh, Pennsylvania, displays popcorn plants in her popcornucopia store window to persuade patrons to purchase popcorn. Paula's popcorn products include crazy caramel corn, chunky cheese corn, nutty walnut corn, pretty sugar-coated popcorn balls and hot-buttered popcorn. It isn't surprising that other popcorn venders fail in comparison to Paula, for she presents a panoramic view of popcorn!

During any particular day, Paula's customers purchased different assortments of popcorn to enjoy at home. On one May day, fifteen patrons each purchased three bags of popcorn at $.75 a bag.

If Paula got to keep only one half of the profits on any given day, how much was her share on that day back in May? (Division, two-digit multiplication, decimals, money)

GA1154

Purely Patriotic Tuesday!

Logical Leader:

Hold an election for class president, vice president, secretary and treasurer. Write a class constitution, complete with laws and amendments. You may also want to include your very own Bill of Rights.

Ask each student to choose one person with qualities which he/she truly admires. Classmates then need to design a bumper sticker with a picture of that person and a few words of wisdom he might express if he were a candidate for public office.

Write a class campaign song for either a real-life or fictional candidate, to the tune of a familiar song like "Old MacDonald Had a Farm" or "Three Blind Mice."

Have each class member write a campaign speech as if he himself was running for a specific office. Include campaign promises as well as consequences if promises aren't met.

Create patriotic puppets by rolling sheets of either red, white or blue butcher paper and taping the ends of the rolls together. Rolls can then be decorated by cutting down into the roll about five inches from the top at two-inch intervals to created "hair," after which twine, feathers, pipe cleaners and other common items can be added to give the puppet its final touches. Markers and crayons can highlight the puppet's facial features and help to make the puppet come alive! Afterwards, scripts can be written to enable puppets to take to the pulpit with their issues.

Invite a local politician in to share his/her experiences in politics with the class. (The mayor, if not too busy, would be an excellent speaking candidate.)

Create a large campaign banner for a real or imaginary candidate. Make sure to provide students with paints, crepe paper and butcher paper with which to design.

GA1154

Purely Patriotic Tuesday!

Lucky Learner:

Make a list of all the items in existence which are red, white and/or blue.

Design invitations for an Inaugural Ball. Decide on the guest list, the menu and don't forget the entertainment! What will guests wear? Draw a scene out of your Inaugural Ball.

Draw political cartoons about some of the more controversial issues which are prevelant today.

Write five solutions to the problem of crooked politicians who use their political contracts to further their crimes.

Design campaign posters and create slogans for fictional storybook and cartoon characters, as well as their offices held.

Examples: Woody Woodpecker for President,
Woody Woodpecker's promises are A-OK!
Watch Woody wash all your cares away!

Take one of the most politically current issues or newspaper stories and turn it into a tall tale.

Create a political collage by pasting pictures of famous politicians onto a large piece of poster board. Give your finished work a title.

Construct a mask of one of your favorite people in the political arena. Use it as you mimic a speech citing his/her views about some major issues.

Brainstorm all the words you can think of when the word *politics* is mentioned. Use those words to design your very own secret word find.

GA1154

Purely Patriotic Tuesday!

Lucky Learner:

Describe the fashion attire which should be worn by both the candidate and his/her spouse during a pep rally.

Write a letter to a specific politician expressing your views and/or opinions about a specific issue.

Create an adventure story about a politician who becomes a national hero for uncovering a smuggling ring and stopping all the "bad guys."

Construct your idea of the "perfect" politician, using only a pencil and paper.

Compose a jingle which could be used on the radio to persuade people to vote for you.

Develop ten possible questions you might ask if you were interviewing a presidential candidate.

Design a campaign button for your choice of presidential candidate.

If this is an election year, illustrate character sketches of each of the presidential candidates.

Invent a skywriting message to be paraded behind either a Democratic or a Republican helicopter.

Create a conversation which might occur between two major presidential candidates.

GA1154

Patriotic Rhyme

One election day in May, a few true patriots began to campaign for more rain. They felt, if the ice wouldn't melt, without rain they would all go insane. So without much ado, they decided to try some VOO-CA-CHOO!

A few little chants towards the sky seemed to pass right by the eye of a tornado named Fredo. A dangling of rain beads made from tulip seeds was another brief try to get the rain to drop by. Their last attempt came with a lion so tame, but he roared in the air without nary a care. No one lied but no matter how hard they tried, the rain didn't come so they sat down and cried!

As they cried and dried and sighed, they each felt a few drops, right on their tops! Yes, at last the rain had come, and now the patriots didn't feel so dumb!

Now here is a question for a dancer and a prancer, and if you're a good thinker, you'll be able to come up with the answer.

If it took 240 drops to get each patriot totally wet, and the rain was dropping at twenty drops per minute, we'll bet—how many minutes before the first patriot was soggy and the last patriot was good and groggy? (Simple division, whole numbers)

GA1154

Red, White and Blue Twisters, Too!

Below you will find three colors—red, white and blue—in honor of all the political celebrations we hold each year in the United States. For each color, you are to write a tongue twister, using as many words as begin with that first letter as possible, and the tongue twister must have something to do with patriotism. One example is given for you to ponder. Have fun and good luck!

RED: Rented Royalty regally removed the rest of the real protesters in response to the rare and irregular regard for the U.S. flag.

RED:

WHITE:

BLUE:

GA1154

Shoes News Day

Logical Leader:

Ask all students to bring to school with them an old discarded shoe and then place the shoes together to create a class sculpture, using string to in some way tie them to one another.

Line everyone in the class in a row and make a comparison, based on shoe sizes, colors and types of shoes being worn.

Design a graffiti board, writing down as many words which relate to shoes as the class can brainstorm. Then turn the words into "shoems" (shoe poems) which can range from limericks to name poems.

Invite a shoe repairman or shoe manufacturer into the classroom to share the processes of shoemaking and shoe repair. Or invite a shoe salesman in to discuss the pros and cons of his/her job.

Read students the poem "Trying on Clothes," by Shel Silverstein from the book *A Light in the Attic*. Ask the class to write similar kinds of poems, but ones which are "solely" about shoes!

Encourage the class to list all the uses for shoes they can possibly think of, from the most realistic to the most fantastic!

Brainstorm as a class as many shoe song titles as possible. Really be imaginative and create puns if at all possible.

Pose the following story starter to the class:

> Samantha the Suede Pump and Terry the Hightops Tennis Shoe were wandering around, looking up at the little boy and his mom as they shopped through the mall. Store after store, Samantha and Terry were stomped on and scuffed and pounded until pretty soon, the shoes decided they weren't going to take it anymore! So they . . . . Now you finish the story.

Ask the class, "If you could be a shoe manufacturer, what one improvement would you make on what specific kind of shoes?"

GA1154

Shoes News Day

Lucky Learner:

Make a list of all the different kinds of shoes there are currently or have been in the past. Categorize them into two columns.

Design the "shoe of the future." Illustrate it in full color and describe its attributes in a paragraph.

Write a conversation which might occur between Sandy the Sandal and Larry the Loafer.

The biggest man ever recorded wore size 37AA (18½") shoes. Write a "tall" tale about a group of young men and women with feet no smaller than size 38.

You've all heard the story about the old lady that lived in a shoe and had so many kids, she didn't know what to do! Fantasize your own story about your fifty brothers and fifty sisters and you and how all of you survive in one small shoe.

Draw a detailed diagram of the shoe you are wearing right now and label all of its parts.

Write three shoe jokes. For example: What did the shoelaces say to the insert? Answer: You'd better hold your tongue or we'll tongue-tie you!

Compose a shoe sonnet entitled "These Shoes Are Made for Hiking."

Write a TV commercial advertising your favorite kind of shoe. You may use the shoe's real name in the ad, but all the other ideas in your commercial must be your own.

GA1154

Shoes News Day

Lucky Learner:

List all of the reasons why a tennis shoe would be more preferable than a high heel if someone wanted to go for a hike up the mountains.

Write an advice column response to the following letter:

Dear Shoes Horse,

I am a model but I unfortunately have very big feet. I always buy shoes two sizes smaller than my feet so they'll look good in front of the cameras. My problem is that my toes are growing together and my feet are swollen and sore all of the time. But if I give up the smaller shoes, I'll have to give up my $600.00 an hour modeling job, too. Oh, what should I do?

Signed,
All Shoes Too Small

The most expensive shoes ever commissioned were pearl-studded shoes from the House of Berluti, Paris, at a cost of $85,000. The most expensive sports shoes ever made and currently available are the mink-lined golf shoes with 18-carat embellishments and ruby-tipped gold spikes at $12,000 a pair. Your job is to design a pair of $25,000 shoes.

Create a flipbook which illustrates a pair of shoes walking down the street when suddenly a dog comes by, and then the shoes step into a puddle.

Imelda Marcos is said to have left her 3000 (later revised to 1060) pairs of shoes in the Filipino Palace when she and her husband fled the country. Design the perfect shoe storage area which could contain up to and over 1000 pairs of shoes.

Develop a logic problem which has to do with three women wearing three different pairs of shoes with three different colored handbags in three different cities. Don't forget the chart!

Design a billboard advertisement for a truly exceptional pair of shoes at a bargain price!

You have just won 100 different pairs of tennis shoes. Describe in one paragraph how you would feel and what you would do with the shoes.

There is a famous song which includes the lyrics "Walk a mile in my shoes . . ." If you could walk a mile in someone else's shoes, whose shoes would you pick and why?

103

GA1154

Socialites Shed Shoes!

Several specialties of shoes were seen right in the middle of the street one scenic day in September. Society socialites swear that the shoes aren't theirs, but their servants say something else. Servants claim the sandals, slippers and gym shoes are indeed the property of the society socialites and that their denial of ownership is super fishy!

It seems that seven pairs of sandals, sixteen pairs of slippers and seventy-six pairs of gym shoes fell from a passing limosine and landed on Sixth Street, just south of Skyline. The shoes were smeared with shades of assorted colors, including chartreuse, sea green, burnt sienna, salmon, spring green, sepia, bittersweet and steele blue.

A seasick sailor even said he saw the socialites throw the shoes, but he wasn't super sure.

So the silly solution to this problem lies in discovering just exactly how many total shoes were seen on Sixth Street that scenic day in September. Can you figure it out? (Simple addition, multiplication, whole numbers)

GA1154

Give 'Em the Shoe Business!

In every business, just like in the shoe business, there are many, many different individuals who collectively make that business work. Shoe businesses start with the original inventor and continue all the way to the individual who purchases the shoe and wears it to the basketball court.

Below are given some of the various individuals who contribute to and directly or indirectly cause the shoe business to flourish. Your job is to first guess, in a sentence or two, what exactly each person's job is, and then to do some research to discover if your answers are correct. Have fun, think hard and good luck!

Shoe company owner:

Shoe designer:

Shoemaker:

Shoe store owner:

Sales promotion (advertising):

Shoe salesperson:

Shoe purchaser and wearer:

Shoeshine boy (or man):

GA1154

Stupendous Sign Day

Logical Leader:

Read to the class the poem "Traffic Light" in Shel Silverstein's book *Where the Sidewalk Ends.* Ask students to think about how much time people spend sitting at signs and lights. Write stories about what life would be like without signs.

Using only the shapes of signs, design a class collage. Name it, and write directions on how to get from one corner to another.

Create a display of the most commonly used signs. Assign each member of the class to be responsible for a different kind of sign.

Take a survey of the class, charting what kinds of signs and how many of each your students have in their neighborhoods.

Have the class decorate cookies with different signs, and create banners in honor of various signs. Hold a sign ceremony, where various members of the class give speeches, stating the many roles signs play in their lives.

Create a class sign mobile, where each student makes a sign out of poster board, cuts it out and adds it to all the others in a hanging tribute to The World of Signs.

Obtain a large map of your city or town. Encourage the class to make a legend for all the signs which could possibly exist. Then use the sign symbols to map out the spots where the signs should go.

Classify all your class neighborhood signs into groups. Use the different categories to write paragraphs which justify each sign's placement into each category.

Have the class write cartoons which feature Wally the One-Way and his confusing first day at Sign School.

GA1154

Stupendous Sign Day

Lucky Learner:

List every single sign and type of sign you can possibly brainstorm.

Invent a new sign which could be used to guard against possible accidents. Design the sign's physical appearance as well as where it should be located.

Write a newspaper article about "The Sign That Came Alive."

Design a comic strip which features Sidney the Stop Sign and Yoda the Yield Sign.

Create a game, using a file folder as a gameboard, which incorporates as many signs as possible for game pieces. (For example, tokens, playing cards, etc.)

Write five solutions each to the problems of speeding and running a red light. In other words, what kinds of things could be done to stop these two from occurring?

Create a large jigsaw puzzle of a stop sign that could even be used by a smaller child.

Write the word *SIGNS* vertically, and using each letter, begin five different words that when put together, create a sentence about signs.

Example:
S igns
I nterest
G rown-ups,
N ot
S quirrels!

Use one of these titles to write a creative story, or invent one of your own:

A Stop Sign Saves a Life
The Three-Way Street Sign
Yield Signs Multiply by the Thousands
Too Many Signs to Handle
Only One Sign Tops the Mountain

GA1154

Stupendous Sign Day

Lucky Learner:

Design a crossword puzzle, using the names of as many signs as possible.

Write three riddles about signs. (Example: I am red and I tell people when to come to a halt. What am I? A stop sign.)

Create an adventure story about Oscar the One-Way Street Sign and his escapades with the hot rods about town.

Design a billboard advertisement about a new sign you've developed.

Develop a logic problem about four different signs on four different streets in four different cities in four different states.

Create awards for classmates in the shapes of different signs.

What would happen if two signs were switched around in your small town? Or your big town? What kinds of situations might occur? What would be the absolutely worst thing that could happen?

The other day, I walked out my front door, got into my car and drove to the end of the street. But when I got there, there were no more street signs, no stoplight, only the faint hint of . . . . Finish the story!

Create a signary (sign dictionary), making a collection of all the signs of which you have knowledge and each of their functions.

What if signs were either male or female? Which signs would fall under which category? Be sure to justify each of your answers.

GA1154

Special Signs Storm St. Sycamore

A sinkful of special signs was found next to a safe and sack of smelling salts in South Sacramento last Sunday. The signs were for safety services, sensible sergeant's seminars, synchronized singing song sanctuaries and samarai sword-throwing contests. Several of the signs symbolized saucy sausages, Saturday saxophone lessons, scaly scalp solutions, scrumptious sweets and scientifically made socks, all for sale.

The social workers seized the signs from Sacramento and shipped them to St. Sycamore in South Savannah. There the special signs were surveyed by seven of the sweetest, most soft-spoken, most secretive and most sedate scientists that St. Sycamore had ever seen.

Now, if each of the scientists surveyed each of the different signs, just exactly how many total times were the special signs surveyed? (Addition, simple multiplication, whole numbers)

GA1154

TV Temptation Tuesday

Logical Leader:

Revise the *TV Guide*! Take ten to twenty shows and have the class rename them and write possible story lines. (Example: *Three's Company* becomes *Eight's a Crowd!* A group of four roommates, two guys and two girls who live on opposite sides of a huge house but share the living quarters in the middle, become too many in this episode as the girls bring home their friends and the guys bring home their friends and pretty soon there's not enough room to sit down in the living room!)

Ask the students to write original TV sitcom scripts which include Wanda the Waitress, Gary the Gardener, Charlie the Chef, Matilda the Maid, and JoJo the Chauffeur with the settings taking place entirely inside a large mansion. Present to the class.

Create TV commercials, in small groups, which advertise products the students create themselves.

Visit a TV studio or invite a TV personality into the classroom to discuss with the students the "behind the scenes" of television.

Show a current TV show to the class and ask them to write critical reviews, citing examples from the program itself.

If your school has a video camera and recorder, encourage the students to tape a half-hour self-produced show complete with commercials and Public Broadcasting messages, which should all be written entirely by themselves.

Do a takeoff of Siskel and Ebert's movie reviews for TV movies. Either review actual movies which have been on television or have students invent their own movies with "thumbs up" or "thumbs down" editorials.

Read "Jimmy Jet and His TV Set" in Shel Silverstein's book *Where the Sidewalk Ends*. Have the class write fantasy poems about what would happen to them if they watched TV as much as Jimmy did.

GA1154

TV Temptation Tuesday

Lucky Learner:

If you were a TV, how many different kinds of things could go wrong to keep you from working? Make a list.

Write the word *TELEVISION* vertically and use each letter to begin a different sentence describing television.

Create a recipe for the perfect TV snack.

What could you do with a television besides watch it?

How would the world be different if TV had never been invented? How would you spend all your spare time? Write a short essay.

One evening, as I was watching my favorite TV show, something really unbelievable happened! As the commercial was about to come on, instead . . . . Now you finish the story.

Design a game strictly for TV lovers which they can play while they are watching TV.

Name fifteen TV actors, ten TV actresses, five TV cartoon characters and one TV comedian whom you admire.

Think about your favorite TV star. What characteristics about him/her do you really enjoy? What are some ways your TV star could improve?

TV Temptation Tuesday

Lucky Learner:

TV's have taken on a whole new look over the past few years. If you could have the perfect TV in your bedroom, what would it have to look like? Illustrate it in its cabinet and be sure to label all the parts.

Brainstorm a list of all the current sitcoms, a list of all the drama shows and a list of all the musical events on TV this past year.

What are all the things TV can be used for besides entertainment? Make a list.

Name twenty ways to spend your time besides watching TV.

If you could watch only one television show for the rest of your life, which one would it be and why? Write an explanatory paragraph.

Invent five new improvements for TV.

If television had one magical quality, what would it be? Why?

GA115

Describe a couch potato in detail and then draw a picture of one.

_____

_____

_____

_____

_____

_____

_____

_____

_____

GA1154

We'll Mix 'Em, You Fix 'Em!

Below are ten scrambled words which all relate to television in some way. The actual words are listed at the bottom of the page. See if you can unscramble each word or word pair. Good luck!

1. cistom

2. posa pareo

3. sivetlonie

4. recstopstars

5. conharnorpes

6. mage hosw

7. yartemocund

8. vemois

9. kalt wosh

10. sewn mate

Word Choices

talk show
sitcom
anchorperson
documentary
soap opera

movies
television
game show
sportscaster
news team

GA115

Wet and Wild Water Wednesday

Logical Leader:

Water conservation is a very important issue today, especially in the drier states. Contact your local water company for the names of the water conservation agencies in your town, and ask for their free brochures to share with the class.

Invite a Culligan man or a Rainbow Water man into your classroom to explain to the class how purified water is made.

Write the words *WATER CONSERVATION* on the chalkboard. Hold a contest to see which student can make the most words out of the letters in *WATER CONSERVATION*. (Example: winter) Give a prize to the student(s) with the most words, the most unusual words and the longest words.

Have students conduct surveys which include the amount of water members of their families and others in the neighborhood use each day, as well as the times when the most water is being utilized. Compare and contrast surveys.

Have the class pantomime how the premier cave dwellers must have looked as they discovered water for the very first time.

Set up microscopes and examine drops of pond water, drinking water from both the tap and the bottle and ocean water, if you get the chance. Have students sketch what they see and then ask them to give their drawings names or titles. Also, discuss the differences and similarities between the different types of water.

At the culmination of this day, line your class up outside in two rows facing one another. Give each pair a water balloon and ask them to stand two feet apart. Now have them toss the water balloon back and forth, getting farther and farther apart until the balloon breaks. This should really cool them off after a fun day's work!

GA1154

Wet and Wild Water Wednesday

Lucky Learner:

Write creative stories, using one of the following titles or one of your own:

       One Hundred Water Balloons Go Pop!
       The Day the Water Was Turned Off
       Water Plus Dirt Equals Mud!
       And Suddenly, Water Became Extinct
       A Drought Hits My Hometown

Water safety is very important to remember as you are having fun in the water. List some safety rules to keep in mind as you are swimming, skiing and boating.

Write the adventure story of Wally the Water Wonderboy and his travels across the ocean, saving aquatic animals and fending off pirates in ships.

Brainstorm at least ten words which mean "wet."

How would you improve a drinking fountain? Design the kind of drinking fountain you might want in your bedroom.

Finish this sentence in at least five different ways:
    Drinking water is like . . . .

What are the properties of water? List them in a paragraph.

Water has been used for many, many different purposes. Brainstorm as many of these uses as you can.

If you could take only one beverage with you into a year's stay on a deserted island, which beverage would it be and why? Write a story about a year with your chosen drink.

GA115

Wet and Wild Water Wednesday

Lucky Learner:

Water trucks spray water over the streets in the summer to keep dust and dirt at a minimum. Research how these trucks work and are made and then redesign the truck to be more efficient.

What would happen if we had no rain for one whole year? Describe the implications for your community and for yourself.

Create a magic water machine which will do a wonderfully imaginative job. Illustrate the machine and explain how it works in a short rhyming poem.

Take the letters from *WET AND WILD WEDNESDAY* and make as many new words as you can. (Example: wilted)

How would you feel if your parents were freshwater fish? Would you respond to them any differently? How would they reinforce the rules? How would they prepare dinner or would they be dinner? Make a list of all the ways your life would change.

Invent five song titles, five book titles and five newspaper headlines which all have to do with water in some way.

As a drop of water, you become friendly with a grain of salt. Describe your relationship in fifty words or less.

Imagine that you have just three wishes as you throw your coin into the wishing well. What wishes would you pick and why those three?

117

GA1154

Warthogs, Warriors and Water

When a wasteland of wonderful wading water was found next to the wagons of wary warriors, they were willing to wash without soap.

The warthogs were wary of the wide-eyed warriors, but the water was clean so they waded in for a wee drink. But what the warthogs and warriors didn't know was that the water was filled with small microscopic creatures called warm-blooded wameoba, who worm their way into your thin wisps of hair and weasel their way into the wax in your ear.

Beware, warthogs and warriors, of the willfull wameoba and watch out for them or they will whisk you away.

And while the wameobas are working on them, you can work out this problem. If every ounce of water the warthogs and warriors drank contained twenty-five wameobas, and they drank twenty gallons of water totally, how many wameobas made their way into the warthogs' and warriors' bodies? (Triple-digit multiplication, whole numbers, measurement)

GA119

Answer Key

Big Billy Bob's Banana Bonanza Page 4
$(12 + 4) \times \$1.00 = \$16.00$

Circus Circumstances Page 15
$10 \times 7 \times 8 \times 175 = 98,000$ citizens

Seeing the USA in a Colorful Way Page 20
$2 + 3 + 3 + 7 + 1 + 1\frac{1}{2} + 8 = 25\frac{1}{2}$ days

Daffy's Delicious Dinner Page 25
$(5 \times 12) + 121 + 83 + 5 + 74 + 4 + 213 = 560$ foods

Dragonalogies Page 30
1. dog; 2. 20; 3. water; 4. kings; 5. whale;
6. dragon; 7. elephant; 8. sword; 9. dragon;
10. criminal

Eggspecially Eggsciting Eggs Page 34
A. $888 \times 88 = 78,144$ eggs
B. $(20 \times 12) \times 88 = 21,120$ eggs
C. $6 + 88 = 94$ is Eggsmond's age
   $8 + 88 = 96$ is Eggsmerelda's age

A Friday Fire Festival Page 39
$110 + 57 + 462 + 54 + 27 + 19 + 309 + 1 + 630 + (5 \times 12) = 1729$ foods

Heroic Heroes Page 48
$7 + 20 + 4 + 10 = 41$ hunks

Rene's Red-Letter Day Page 54
$(3 + 4 + 5 + 1) + 1 + 1 + 20 + 1 + 1 + 1 + 1 + 1 + 56 + 19 + (2 + 12 + 26 + 10) = 165$ red things

Isabel Screams for Ice Cream! Page 59
$142 + 57 + 29 + 62 + 11 + 33 + 71 + 54 + 16 + 28 + 4 + 25 = 532$ gallons

Ice-Cream Delight Page 60

Monster Madness Page 69
$(1 + 327) \times 4 \div 16 = 82$ pounds

Naturally Nutty Page 74
$7 \times 27 = 189$ dances

A Pizza Problem Eats Away! Page 89
Patty likes sausage, stays two hours and listens to PAL; Pixie likes cheese, stays four hours and listens to Pinkey Lee; and Penelope likes pepperoni, stays six hours and listens to Pasley Meadow.

Lucky Pizza Day! Page 90
$1 + 2 + 3 + 4 + 5 + 6 + 7 + 8 + 9 + 10 = 55$ pizzas

Paula Peacock's Popcorn Products Page 95
$(15 \times 3 \times .75 \div 2 = \$16.88$

Patriotic Rhyme Page 99
$240 \div 20 = 12$ minutes

Socialites Shed Shoes! Page 104
$(7 + 16 + 76) \times 2 = 198$ shoes

Special Signs Storm St. Sycamore Page 109
$9 \times 7 = 63$ times

We'll Mix 'Em, You Fix 'Em! Page 114
1. sitcom; 2. soap opera; 3. television;
4. sportscaster; 5. anchorperson; 6. game show; 7. documentary; 8. movies; 9. talk show;
10. news team

Warthogs, Warriors and Water Page 118
$25 \times 128 \times 20 = 64,000$ wameobas

119

GA1154

Bibliography

*A special thanks to these authors and publishers, for without their inspirational and supplemental ideas, this book could not have been written.

Bagley, Michael T., and Karin K. Hess. *200 Ways of Using Mental Imagery in the Classroom*. Trillium Press, 1984.

Foley, Kathy U., Mara Lud, and Carol Power, *The Good Apple Guide to Creative Drama*. Carthage, IL: Good Apple, Inc., 1981.

Guinness Book of World Records, Bantam Books, 1988.

McGee-Cooper, Ann. *Building Brain Power*. Zephyr Press, 1982.

Silverstein, Shel. *A Light in the Attic*. Harper and Row, 1981.

_____. *Where the Sidewalk Ends*. Harper and Row, 1974.

Stanish, Bob. *Sunflowering*. Carthage, IL: Good Apple, Inc., 1977.

_____. *The Unconventional Invention Book*, by Bob Stanish, Carthage, IL: Good Apple, Inc., 1981.

Wayman, Joe, and Lorraine Plum. *Secrets & Surprises*. Carthage, IL: Good Apple, Inc., 1977.

The Yellow Pages for Students and Teachers. From the kid's stuff people. Incentive Publications, 1980.

GA11